CW00520789

Edward Anders

Amidst Latvians During the Holocaust

I. Autobiography 1926–1949

II. Latvians During WWII:
An Evenhanded Analysis

Occupation Museum Association of Latvia

Rīga, 2010

ii

Occupation Museum Association of Latvia, Rīga

Latvijas Okupācijas muzeja biedrība (OMB), Rīga

© 2010 by Edward Anders. All rights reserved

ISBN 978-9984-9931-8-8

To my Latvian Compatriots,
In the hope
That the Lessons of the Past
Will Help Latvia Become
A United, Happy, Prosperous Nation!

CONTENTS

vi

PREFACE

When Stalin brutally seized Latvia—my country—in June 1940, I was one of many Latvian patriots alarmed at this perfidious aggression. I narrowly escaped deportation to the USSR on 14 June 1941. But a few days later when Hitler attacked the Soviet Union and swiftly drove the Red Army out of Latvia, I became one of 90,000 Latvian Jews who suddenly faced death. The Holocaust began at once. Jews were shot by tens, hundreds, and thousands. Only 2% survived the Nazi occupation.

I am one of them. This is my story.

My father invented an audacious bluff to save his wife and sons—though not himself. My mother was to claim that she was a German foundling raised by Jewish parents. At best this bluff would last a few months, as too many people in our town (Liepāja, pop. 57,000) knew our family. Against all odds, we managed to stretch it out for 2 years, followed by a few years in legal limbo when we "slipped through cracks in the Holocaust". My mother and I survived, though my father, brother, and 24 other relatives perished.

Not having been in ghettos or camps, I evaded the horrendous suffering of most other survivors. That makes my survival story less dramatic, if more unusual. However, I had a unique vantage point. Whereas other survivors lived behind barbed wire, tormented by their captors, I was able to live and work among ordinary people, watching their responses to the war, the Nazi occupation, and the Holocaust. Like some other survivors I saw shades of gray where others—and the Moscow propaganda machine—see only pitch black.

Being well known in my field of science for an elephantine memory, I recall the war years in great detail. I recently recorded my reminiscences in a memoir distributed only to family and a few friends. At the urging of several friends I have now edited and condensed the 1926–1949 section (**Part I**) for wider distribution. But I have also added a section (**Part II**) on the Latvian people during WWII—a period when the country was nearly sealed off from the world by its occupiers' news blackout.

The picture I present is full of the nuances, surprises, and ambiguities of life as it is really lived. I offer it in a spirit of tolerance and bridge building.

Edward Anders

Part I.
Autobiography 1926–49

1. THE DECEMBER MASSACRE

MY FATHER Adolf was shot on 9 December 1941. A week earlier, the police had found him hiding in our apartment and arrested him and my mother. She was released but he was executed by a firing squad.

As it turned out, he would have been killed 6 days later anyway. *SS-Einsatzgruppe A* under *SS-Brigadeführer* (Brigadier General) Walter Stahlecker had killed about half of the ~300,000 Jews in the Baltics by late October. But this pace was not fast enough for Himmler, who transferred his most accomplished henchman—*SS-Obergruppenführer* (Lieutenant General) Friedrich Jeckeln, who had organized the murder of 36,000 Jews at Babi Yar, Ukraine—to the Baltics in mid-November. On 30 November and 8 December ~25,000 Jews were killed at Rumbula near Rīga, and on 15 December it was the turn of my hometown Liepāja.

The local paper carried a notice that Jews were not to leave their homes on December 14–16, but we thought it didn't concern us. Early during the German occupation, our mother Erica had managed to persuade the Security Police chief Kügler that she was not the biological child of her Jewish parents but a German foundling. He had issued special passes to my brother and me, certifying us as half-Jews: second-class citizens but exempt from most anti-Jewish rules.

At 4 AM on 15 December I was awakened by the light going on in my bedroom. When I opened my eyes, I saw two Latvian policemen standing in the room, rifles over their shoulders. They told brother Georg and me to get dressed and follow them. Three others searched the apartment for Adolf who was also on their list; a sixth stood behind the back door to block any escape attempt. They refused to tell us where they were taking us, but the oldest one finally suggested we wear warm clothes. Knowing that we were headed for a mass grave, we protested and showed our passes, but this talisman had suddenly lost its power. Yet the police would not take Erica, who demanded to go with us.

It took us about 2½ hours to reach the town's Women's Prison, only 10 blocks away. Every block or so we had to stop, facing the wall. A few of the rifle-armed policemen stayed behind to guard us, while the others entered the house to round up Jewish families (mainly women and children, as most men had been shot in July). Some of the arrested Jews still clung to the hope that they would be deported; I recall a mother lamenting to her children that she had forgotten to take along her husband's picture. Among those rounded up was our great-aunt Johanna Ginsburg, the dearest of our relatives. She pretended not to know us but sighed deeply when she saw us.

We kept up a running argument with the policemen guarding us, protesting that our passes exempted us from such arrests. One young policeman turned livid at our insubordination, and, after cursing us with a blast of anti-Semitic invective, asked the sergeant whether it was all right to shoot us on the spot (2 blocks from our house), as a warning to the others. We did not hear the sergeant's reply, but it calmed him down for the time being.[1]

Our little troop grew to perhaps 40 people, and as we approached the jail, we saw similar columns emerge from side streets. We had no illusions as to what was in store for us, and neither did our mother, who tried to join first our group and then another, having been driven away by the guards.

We were among the last to arrive at the jail and were ordered to line up near the gate, facing the wall (Fig. 1). It was still quite dark at this time (6:30–7:00 AM) because in Liepāja the sun does not rise until almost 9 in mid-December, but the yard was brightly lit by floodlights. Some 500 Jews were gathered there, listening attentively as a German policeman called roll. He had already reached letter K by the time we arrived.

1. Old Gates of the Women's Prison, From Yard Side

The Latvian gatekeeper urged us in a chummy whisper to give him our watches, jewelry, or any other valuables. We were to be deported to Germany, he said, where such things would be

---

[1] We were lucky not to be living in Rīga. There over 1,000 Jews were shot during roundup in the ghetto or on the march to the Rumbula execution site, for resisting, refusing to go, falling behind, etc. Andrew Ezergailis, *The Holocaust in Latvia, 1941–1944: The Missing Center*. Rīga: Historical Institute of Latvia, 1996, Ch. 8 (hereafter cited as Ezergailis, *Holocaust*).

taken away from us. And wasn't it better to leave them with our fellow countrymen instead?

Soon there was a commotion at the gate. Erica, who had finally managed to get into the prison yard with another column, had been recognized and was being pushed out into the street. She had gone to German *Schutzpolizei* (order police) headquarters, a block from the jail, where she pleaded with an officer to release us. He seemed sympathetic, but when he heard that we had been arrested at 4 AM, he said it was already too late. It was then about 7 AM.

A few minutes later, several of the Latvian policemen who had arrested us approached with a German *Schutzpolizist* from Danzig in the lead. He asked us for our side of the story; we told him that our mother was German and showed him our passes. He stared at us for a very long 5 seconds (presumably running through his checklist of Jewish racial characteristics), and then dismissed us with the single word "*geht*" (go), while motioning to the watch collector to let us out.

The gate opened, we stepped out on the street, and nearly bumped into our mother. Thinking us dead, she was trying once more to get into the jail to share our fate.

We had been perfectly calm during the 3½ hours since our arrest, though we knew where we were headed. But now that we were free, we got a good case of the shivers. It was over by the time we got home for a quick breakfast, and then Georg went off to work. He was an hour late that day, and I am not sure what excuse he offered. We did not dwell on this experience, focusing instead on the challenges of the day and the hour. The next day, as I crossed the bridge separating the old and new parts of town, I saw a group of some 20 Jewish men walking across under police guard, heading north to the Šķēde execution site, 11 km away. We had eluded this fate, but for how long?

A few of the other prisoners in that yard survived, saved by German Navy Administrative Inspector (1st Lieutenant) Friedrich Kroll. He was in charge of the Navy's Uniform Warehouse in the former Cork Factory where about 100 Jews worked. When he found that many of his workers had been arrested, he rushed off to prison with 2 of his aides, got an SS-man to announce that anyone working in the Cork Factory should step forward, and led them out of the prison. Even a few Jews who did not work at the Cork Factory had the presence of mind to join the group and then quietly drift away once they were on the street. Kroll urged his workers not to go home the next 2 days but to sleep in the Cork Factory. Still, he repeated his prison visits the next 2 days and rescued a number of Jews.[2]

For 3 days, the victims were marched or driven in small groups to the former Latvian army target range Šķēde, 11 km north of the prison, where they were shot. Since the start of the German occupation, there had been rumors giving details of these executions, and these rumors multiplied in December. The executioners allegedly were given a liter of vodka a day for their labors; they had recently been ordered by headquarters to aim two bullets at the head rather than one at the head and one at the heart; etc. A carter at the construction company where I later worked reported seeing victims lining up in a row at the top of a dune, and then toppling over after a salvo like bowling pins. That is confirmed by pictures of the executions at http://www.liepajajews.org/shkede_web/index.html

We had eluded death, by the whim of a German policeman. But our chances of surviving WWII now were greatly diminished, as the Security Police passes had suddenly become worthless. The best we could hope for was that we would have a chance to argue our claim of Erica's "Aryan blood" before some other German official. But by now, 6 months after the occupation, German officials had become very leery of such claims by desperate Jews. Indeed, our classmates Georg and Eduard Spektor and their parents, who had similarly claimed the mother to be Aryan, had been shot after they overplayed their hand by trying to save the father.

---

[2] In 2003 I nominated Kroll to Yad Vashem for recognition as "Righteous Among the Nations", but although I had the support of 4 survivors and written confirmation of the rescue in a Holocaust diary by Kalman Linkimer, Yad Vashem turned it down. I learned that their standards for German military are very stringent, requiring proof of great personal risk. I sent them a document showing that one of Kroll 's fellow officers, Dr. Lancelle, who had merely called the killing of Jews "murder", was court-martialed, demoted to private, and assigned to combat duty in a penal unit. But that was not enough for Yad Vashem.

Fortunately we did not know that the war would last another 1240 days. As we were to discover, survival required several miracles, plenty of luck, and the right decision at critical moments—by instinct, chance, or wits.

2. BACKGROUND

WAS BORN on 21 June, 1926, in Liepāja (German: Libau), Latvia, as the second son of Adolf and Erika Alperovitch (Alperovičs).[3] My father, an Anglophile, chose English names for me and my older brother, Georg. Father worked in my grandfather's grain export business and grain mill, which he was soon to inherit; Mother kept the ledgers but otherwise did not work.

HOME TOWN

Liepāja (pop. 57,000 in 1939) had been a bustling naval and commercial port in the Russian Empire, being its only ice-free outlet on the Baltic. (In the 1904/5 Russian-Japanese war, the

---

[3] For person names, I use the spelling preferred by the individual or descendants during their lifetime, but transliterated into English as needed. Most Latvian Jews had at least 3 first names: an official, usually Hebrew name; an unofficial, usually secular name, and a nickname or diminutive used by the family. Surnames had similar variety, reflecting the dominant language at the time. Names ending in –vitch (a Slavic suffix meaning "son of") could be spelled –vich (Russian), -witz (German) or –vičs (Latvian). More variety was caused by differences among alphabets. Russian has no H and substitutes G for it; Latvian has no W or Y and uses V and I instead; German has both W and V but pronounces them like an English V and F, respectively.

Russian fleet that was so disastrously defeated at Tsushima had
sailed from Liepāja). During WWI, the Germans quickly
captured Liepāja in their 1915 spring offensive, as the wooden
decoys that the Russians had placed in the seashore forts to
supplement real guns were deficient in firepower. After Latvian
independence in 1918 Liepāja, shrunk to only half its pre-war
population, declined in importance. But it still prospered as a
major fishing and commercial port for Latvian and Soviet
exports and imports, as well as a trade and industrial center.

Scenically, Liepāja was not a major tourist attraction. The
turn-of-the-century, *Jugendstil* buildings in Old-Liepāja (south of
the harbor canal) were too new in my youth to be of interest.
New-Liepāja (a poorer, partly industrial section north of the
canal) and the Naval Base (still further north) had even less
appeal. But Liepāja had a beautiful, gently sloping beach with
fine, white sand, bordered by willow bushes or pines some 50
meters from the shore. Especially after a storm, one could gather
seashells, amber, and other flotsam. The Baltic has only ¼ the
salinity of the world's major oceans, which is a boon to klutzy
swimmers with poor breathing technique. Even the jellyfish that
appeared every August were benign, incapable of stinging.

The economy was labor-intensive: there was a single
department store with a medium-sized supermarket, but most
people bought their food at the daily farmers' market after
comparing the offerings at various stands, or at the many small
grocery, dairy, or bakery stores. There were clothing and shoe
stores, but those people who could afford it had their clothes
custom-made by the many tailors in town. For local
transportation, there were a couple of street car lines, lots of
horse cabs, and—for upscale travelers—a number of taxis,
including some late US models. Train service was good but
s-l-o-w; the 230 km trip to the capital, Rīga, took 5 hours. Plane
services, established shortly before WWII, cut it to 1 hr. Private
cars were few and far between (I would guess 50–100, or about
one for every 1,000 people), as were telephones (about 2,000) and
refrigerators. Our family was extremely immobile by US
standards; we children went to Rīga only about once a year, and
except for summer camp, never to other towns in Latvia.

Life moved at a leisurely pace. There were parks and promenades where people went for evening or weekend strolls. There also was a soccer stadium, tennis and yacht clubs, etc.

Culturally, Liepāja did not do badly for a small town. It had about half a dozen movie houses, a theater that also performed operas (in Latvian!), summer concerts at a band shell in the park, and a decent public library. No doubt there were other cultural activities that I was not aware of.

Germans had colonized Latvia since the middle of the 12th century, and Baltic-German barons retained cultural and economic dominance even after the Livonian War (1558–1582), when Sweden, Poland, and Russia fought over Latvia and divided the spoils. Courland, comprising the two westernmost provinces of Latvia, became a German duchy under Polish suzerainty (1562–1795), and even after its subsequent annexation by Russia (Fig. 2), the Baltic-German barons kept their privileges and their German-language parliament. As late as 1863, when Liepāja had grown to a population of ~11,000, 70% of the residents were German. Although the percentage of ethnic Germans eventually dropped to ~10% as the town grew to about 100,000 by migration from other parts of Latvia and from Russia, German remained the preferred language of the educated classes, even after intensive russification efforts by Tsar Alexander III (1881–1893).

The minority population had dropped considerably by the end of WWI, and with Latvia's independence in 1918, Latvian became the official language. I am not sure about Liepāja, but in some parts of Latvia the transition did not go smoothly, as minorities were slow to accept the fact that the former "peasant folk" now ruled the land. Street signs in Liepāja still were in 3 languages—Latvian, German, and Russian—until 1933, when rising nationalism caused them to be replaced by Latvian signs. The nationalistic dictatorship (1934–1940) under US-educated Kārlis Ulmanis further enforced the primacy of Latvian and made English rather than German the foreign language in schools from second grade on.

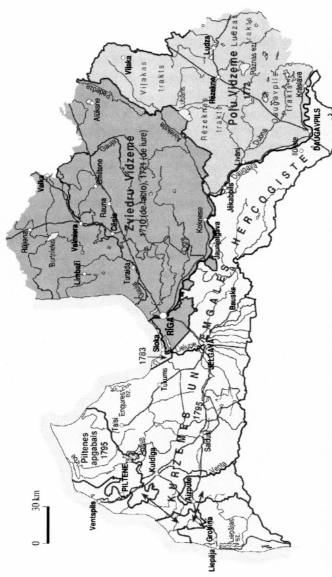

Latvia in the 18th century, showing annexations by Russia. **Swedish Vidzeme** (*Zviedru Vidzeme*), including Riga, was captured by Peter the Great in 1710. **Latgale** (*Poļu Vidzeme*) came next, at the First Partition of Poland in 1772. The **Courland Duchy** (*Kurzemes un Zemgales Hercogiste*) was last, at the Third Partition of Poland in 1795. It included the 3 non-contiguous parts of the **Piltene District**, an early settlement region for Jews. (© Jāņa sēta, Riga, 1998).

Fig. 2.

JEWS OF LATVIA

Until the 19th century, Jews in Latvia were largely restricted to the easternmost province, Latgale, which had been under Polish-Lithuanian rule since 1581 (Fig. 2). The kings of Poland had tolerated, even welcomed, immigration of Jews expelled from Western countries since the late Middle Ages, and a number of these Jews fled to Latgale after the massacres by Ukrainian Cossacks during their 1648–1653 uprising led by Khmelnytsky. When Latgale was annexed to Russia in the first partition of Poland (1772), Empress Catherine the Great included it in the "Pale of Settlement" (Ukraine and Byelorussia) where Jews were allowed to live, being largely banned from Russia proper. A much smaller number of Jews, mainly from Germany, had trickled into the Courland Duchy since the 16th century, and lived either in its capital Jelgava (Mitau) or in the Piltene District (the former Courland Bishopric—3 non-contiguous areas connected by double arrows in Fig. 2) that was under direct Polish rule and more open to Jewish immigration.

In contrast to the Russian-oriented Latgale Jews, the Courland Jews were German-oriented. During the 1855–1881 reign of liberal Tsar Alexander II (who emancipated the serfs in Russia and started liberal reforms in Finland) residence restrictions were temporarily relaxed for Jews in "useful" occupations, such as MDs, merchants, and artisans. Jews from Latgale and other parts of the Pale migrated into the previously closed parts of Latvia until Alexander III reimposed the restrictions in 1882. In 1939, Latvia had 4.4% Jews and Liepāja, 13%.

Anti-Semitism was strong in Tsarist Russia, and became violent at times. After the assassination of Alexander II in 1881, there were hundreds of pogroms in Ukraine, Byelorussia, and Russia proper (but none in Latvia), triggered by the false rumor that the assassins were Jews. Smaller-scale pogroms often occurred at Easter, in revenge for the killing of Christ. These were spontaneous outbursts by the masses (sometimes encouraged by priests or government agents), but anti-Semitism permeated the Russian government as well. The Tsarist secret police (Okhrana) in the late 1890s produced a forgery, *Protocols of the Elders of Zion,* purporting to be a secret plot by Jews to achieve world domination. It was translated into many languages, was widely distributed by the Nazis to justify persecution of Jews, and is still cherished by neo-Nazis and Moslem extremists to justify anti-Semitism and genocide.

Jews often served as scapegoats, for example in WWI, when German troops invaded Courland in May 1915, swiftly seized Liepāja on May 8, and approached Jelgava. The Russian Army Commander, Grand Duke Nikolai Nikolayevich, accused Jews of spying for the German army, signaling to the Germans, and hiding German soldiers caught behind the front lines. He therefore ordered Jews to leave Courland within 24 hours. Thus some 40,000 Courland Jews, with little more than the clothes on their backs, were deported in boxcars to the Russian interior, often forced to continue on foot. Many perished, and only ~17,000 returned after the war. No wonder that some 1,200 young Jews joined the Latvian National Army in the independence war 1918–1920.

As in all European countries east of the Rhine, Jewishness in Latvia, Russia, Poland, etc. was defined not merely by religion but by blood. The term was "nationality", meaning ethnicity, not citizenship. It did not matter for how many generations the family had lived in the country or how well they had assimilated: Jews remained Jews, (Baltic) Germans remained Germans, etc. All were classified as "minorities". Russia (and later the USSR) went farthest in this respect, recording nationality and religion not only in (domestic) passports but also in school diplomas. USSR passports had "nationality" as question 5, stigmatizing Jews as implied in a joke about a want ad placed by a Jew: "Trade question 5 for two criminal offenses".

Latvia did not list nationality or religion in passports or diplomas, but asked for them in censuses and certain application forms. At the insistence of the League of Nations, Latvia gave generous "cultural autonomy" rights to its minorities, permitting them to run schools in their own language at government expense. In the late 1930s, 85% of Jewish children of elementary school age attended Jewish schools where the language of instruction was Yiddish or Hebrew. The minorities felt no pressure to assimilate and gladly built up their own cultural life, walled off from other minorities and from Latvians. There were Jewish newspapers, theaters, political parties, etc.—even soccer clubs, sports clubs, boy scout troops—and as Jews voted mainly for their own parties, they always had adequate representation in parliament. (The most distinguished Jewish deputy, Prof. Max Laserson, later criticized the other Jewish deputies for remaining silent in parliamentary debates unless these involved subjects of interest to Jews). Many young Jews were Zionists, with their bodies in Latvia but their hearts in Palestine. Friendships between Jews and Latvians were rare, and so was perfect command of the Latvian language. This self-segregated life was very comfortable, but prevented buildup of strong solidarity between Latvians and Jews.

MY PARENTS

My paternal grandfather **Israel** (1862–1934) was born in Kurenets, Byelorussia and came to Liepāja only in 1878, at a time when many Byelorussian Jews moved to Latvia after the railway line from Romny (Ukraine) to Liepāja had been completed in 1876. The families of my other 3 grandparents had been living in Latvia since at least the late 18th century—the farthest I have been able to trace them.

As far as I know, **Father Adolf (Aba) Alperovitch** (1897–1941; Fig. 3) had a happy youth. Set for a career in his father's grain export business, he attended the Russian-language "Business High School" (*Kommerzschule*) in Liepāja, graduating with respectable grades in 1914. He had intended to go to university—I found a visiting card listing him as an engineering student—but WWI broke out two months after his graduation. Being only 17 at the start of the war he was not drafted, and less than a year later, before he had reached military age, the Germans drove the Russians out of Courland. In that war the German occupation was no hardship; father worked in grandfather's business and had enough time after hours to socialize and have fun with his friends.

Father's older brother, **Hermann** (1893–1940) studied at the Berlin Polytechnic Institute from ~1913, but then somehow got to St. Petersburg during or after the Bolshevik revolution and—despite his bourgeois background—became a committed Communist. He was reporter or editor at 7 regional papers of the Communist party from 1918 to March 1937, when he was arrested in Stalin's purges on the ludicrous charge of being a German spy. Another reason may have been an anti-corruption pamphlet *"On Restoring the Health of the Party"* that he had published in 1921. He died in 1940 of injuries allegedly suffered when on his way to interrogation he jumped out of the window and fell on (a fence of?) sharp metal pikes.

3., 4. Father Adolf (~1914) and mother Erica (~1916).

Mother **Erica (Rachel) Sheftelovitch-Meiran** (1895–1992; Fig. 4) had a much less happy youth, according to her. As the third daughter of parents who presumably had been hoping for a son, she felt neglected and unloved, particularly by her mother. She was jealous of her older sisters **Hedwig** (1891–1930) and **Lili** (1893–1927), especially the former. Erica attended the private girls' *Gymnasium* of A. E. Gessau from 1907 to 1916, graduating with middling grades. After the Germans took Liepāja in May 1915, she worked as a clerk in the district office (*Kreisamt*) of the

German military administration. She was quite a beauty, and after she met my father in June 1917, both fell deeply in love. But Adolf's parents were opposed to their marriage, objecting to Erica's family on grounds of personal incompatibility, social status, or both. Adolf and Erica finally got married in 1919, but the two sets of in-laws avoided each other and never met socially.

My parents spoke Russian to each other during courtship and the early years of marriage, and even my **brother Georg** (1924–1944) started out with Russian. But soon after I was born, my parents switched to German, using Russian only when they did not want us children to understand. Both also spoke Latvian (Erica with an accent). They knew Yiddish but rarely used it.

Father was intelligent and well read, but rather reserved, aloof, and touchy. Mother was less intellectual and very impulsive, short-tempered, and impatient. But in contrast to Father, she thrived on people, knew how to use her looks and charm to advantage, and was a good actress. For this reason he occasionally sent her on important errands to banks or government agencies (e.g., to get an export license). Whereas Father was a "straight arrow", one of whose mottoes was "The best lie is the truth", Mother had no great qualms about bending the truth, even for minor advantage.

Both my parents socialized mainly with other Jews. Most of Father's contacts were through business, and as much of business was in Jewish hands, his narrow focus was understandable. Erica also had mainly Jewish friends, except for her Baltic German childhood friend Ella Woita (in Rīga) and Elza Grīnvalds, the wife of an upper class Latvian shipping magnate. Erica believed that one should always pick friends of higher status from whom one could learn, and the Grīnvalds family definitely met that standard. Their well-bred, well-mannered sons, Jānis Puriņš (from her first marriage) and Gvīdo, often were held up to us as models to be emulated, but we somehow lacked the zeal to rise to this challenge.[4]

---

[4] Jānis seemed destined for a diplomatic career, but when I last talked to him in the winter of 1943/44, he wore the uniform of the Latvian Legion. From his widow who contacted me after reading this book I learned that he had survived the war and died in 1995. His younger half-brother Gvīdo also survived, became a sea captain and lived in Denmark in 2010.

Except during my early years, we rarely entertained guests at home; whether due to custom, finances, or my father's aloofness. Both parents met their friends in cafés or restaurants. Georg and I may have been taken to a café a very few times, but I do not recall ever being taken to a restaurant, at least in Liepāja. Nor did all 4 of us ever go on vacations together; at most, we two boys accompanied Mother on a trip.

Some of my most uncomfortable memories of that time concern treatment of lower social classes. Erica went through a huge number of cooks/maids, scolding, abusing, mocking, and firing them for minor reasons. Even before the Depression, Latvia was a buyer's market for household help, and Erica seemed unconcerned that the poor maid she fired might not find another job for months and become an anti-Semite. Once in 1931 or 1932 an old man appeared in the yard of our apartment building and without asking sawed and split the firewood logs that were piled up in a corner. (Although our building had central heat, the kitchen stoves were wood-burning.) The job finished, he came to our door and politely asked to be paid. Angrily, my mother chased him away despite his pleas, as she had not hired him to do the job. I felt very sorry for him and still vividly remember the scene.

A few years later, perhaps 1934 or 1935, I began to visit Grandpa's grain mill, where I befriended one of the workers who showed me the big steam engine and the banks of noisy machines that ground grain, sifted flour, etc. I was shocked to learn a few months later that my father had fired my buddy. The offense? He had walked into the office one Friday afternoon when the payroll was late and asked in a slightly fresh tone, "What's the matter, won't we get paid today?"

3. GROWING UP IN LIEPĀJA

PROSPERITY, 1919–1935

THE TWENTIES were a prosperous time for my family. Grandfather Israel's grain mill and export business flourished. Father worked in grandfather's businesses and apparently had a comfortable income. Grandma Henna and daughter Ida—often if not always accompanied by my mother— spent several weeks every year in the fashionable Karlovy Vary (Karlsbad) spa in Czechoslovakia. They also took train trips to Germany, Lithuania, and a few other countries. Foreign travel was expensive in those days, so only the wealthy could afford it.

The Years Before School

We lived in a 7-room apartment in a very nice neighborhood (Lorenz St., now Krišjāna Barona St., 8), 200 yards from the park and school and 500 yards from the beach. Of two rare luxuries in Liepāja buildings—central heat and running hot water—the building had only the former, but it also had a huge garden and a yard with a sandlot. Like other upper-middle class families, we had a maid and a German governess, as well as a nursemaid while I was small. Both my parents were avid tennis players and belonged to the local club.

These were carefree years. Our social life was quite active while we lived in that apartment, much more so than in later ones. We often saw aunt Ida and her husband Arthur who lived in the same building, and we children had big birthday parties for a dozen or more guests. One picture (Fig. 5) shows me seated on a garden chair, surrounded by my guests and their governesses. I alone made a sour face, because the photographer made me take off my paper hat whereas the guests could keep theirs. Illustrating the usual self-isolation, all but one of the children were Jewish.

5. *My 4ᵗʰ birthday party, with paper hats and Latvian flags. The tall boy right behind me is "role model" Jānis Puriņš, Georg is to his right, and cousin Herbert is on the far right, with his governess behind him. Our governess, Ms. Popov, is on the far left. Erica is in the middle. (June 1930).*

For several years, Father strongly favored my older brother. One reason was that I was an unplanned child; another, that I was not very lovable. I was skinny, small, stubborn, and short-tempered, as well as pale and sickly (rickets and rheumatic fever, along with the usual childhood diseases). Father also was not the most even-handed arbiter of our squabbles. When I said that Georg had started the fight, the verdict was "but you finished it", and we were both punished. But if I had started the fight, the verdict was "you pipsqueak, you have no business starting a fight with your big brother", and I got most or all of the punishment. Perhaps this was all to the good, as it got me thinking about fairness and justice.

Georg and I got along fairly well with each other, despite occasional fights. Both of us had long eyelashes, and one day Georg declared that he was tired of looking at the world through hair. He trimmed his eyelashes with scissors, and mine as well— presumably even before his own, to perfect his technique.

I was starved for my father's love and approval. He called my brother but not me by a diminutive, and when he finally did so (I was about 5 then) I rushed into the next room and excitedly told my mother. I overheard her telling this to my father, and I think that's when he became friendlier and fairer toward me. Indeed, from age 12 or so our relationship became positively warm. Child rearing in our part of the world was still done without help from psychology or how-to books.

Toys, Pranks, House Rules

Among the toys I played with at age 3 was a cardboard puzzle with a picture on one side and letters of the alphabet on the other. My governess must have explained them to me, because one morning in my parents' bedroom, I looked at their 1920's vintage radio and to their surprise read out the name *"Neutrodyn"* (not all that hard, as German is a phonetic language). It took me much longer to learn how to write. Indeed, most of my secretaries claim I never did.

Our governess took us for walks whenever the weather permitted. During the summer we spent hours at the beach, building sand castles in the fine white sand. The park along the seashore, less than 2 blocks away, also was a delightful place in all seasons. In the winter we rode our sled in the park, either on the level or downhill.

In retrospect I realize that the German proverbs that our governesses recited (without reference to religion) whenever our moral fiber needed strengthening, eventually had a beneficial effect on us. Here are some examples, which unfortunately lose their rhyme and some of their impact in English translation.

- *Duty first, then pleasure*
- *Lies have short legs*
- *Self-praise stinks*

- *Lie once and people won't believe you,*
  even when you tell the truth
- *Don't do unto others what you don't want done*
  unto yourself

Evenings at home were pleasant. Radio provided only news but no entertainment; TV was unknown, and 78-rpm records (at 4 min a side), played on a hand-cranked player, provided only brief entertainment. Thus our favorite pastimes were books and games, such as dominoes, checkers, bingo, children's card games, tin soldiers, etc. Adults very occasionally played roulette (for penny stakes), which we were allowed to join. On New Year's eve, we poured molten lead into water and tried to predict our fortunes from the bizarre shapes.

We had to eat the food placed before us, whether we liked it or not, and for vitamin D we also had to take the truly disgusting cod liver oil. There were only a few dishes I strongly disliked (salt herring, head cheese, fried sausage), but my parents gave no quarter. One evening shortly before supper my mother noticed a bulge in my cheek and discovered some well-chewed meat from lunch that I hadn't had the stamina to swallow or the sense to spit out. Eventually I learned to deposit such "morsels" under furniture.

Rules were equally strict about clothing. My skin is very sensitive even to soft wool, and thus I was in agony when at age ~8 I received very heavy, very coarse, and undoubtedly very warm socks and gloves, hand-knitted from carpet-grade wool. They felt like nettles if not poison ivy. I surreptitiously tried wearing cotton socks underneath, but was caught, ridiculed, and forced to wear the wool socks without a liner. I had a few *very* uncomfortable days before my parents relented.

Elementary School

When Georg entered the nearby (German) Reimers school[5] in early 1931, I wanted to go, too. My parents said that I was too young and couldn't get up early enough, but when I rose with Georg every morning and then stood at the door with a long face

---

[5] There were 3 German elementary schools in Liepāja, and several Jewish schools.

as he left for school, they finally relented and enrolled me in early 1932. In retrospect, I think I was motivated as much by sibling rivalry as by thirst for knowledge.

I knew about grades but was hazy about student prerogatives, so when the teacher returned my first penmanship exercise with a grade of 2 (D), I indignantly crossed it out and wrote in a 5 (A). She took me aside, put her hand on my shoulder, and gently explained to me how the grading system worked.

Hitler still was a few months away from taking power in Germany, but his anti-Semitism began to infect some Baltic Germans while the Latvian government became increasingly nationalistic, asserting the primacy of its language. Although some 85% of Jewish children attended Jewish elementary schools, my parents transferred me to the (Latvian) *Čakste* school in the fall of 1932. That was a fateful decision, which helped me survive the Holocaust. I spoke no Latvian at that time (like most prosperous Courland Jews, we spoke German at home), but learned it with the usual facility of a 6-year old.

Latvian schools in those days were very good but tough by US standards of ~2000. Classes were co-ed only through the 3rd grade; they were large (35–40), and promotion was not automatic. Pupils who failed one subject had to take a special exam at the end of summer and could go on to the next grade only if they passed. In more marginal cases they merely had to complete a huge "summer assignment" for promotion. Those who failed more than one subject had to repeat a grade. Only elementary school (6+1 grades) was mandatory, so pupils who were well below average got special, restricted diplomas that did not entitle them to apply to high school. (Even students with a regular diploma still had to pass entrance exams in two subjects to gain admission).

The school did not provide textbooks; we bought our own. Ballpoint pens had not yet been invented, so we wrote with steel pens dipped into inkbottles that were provided in each of our forms. My grades in elementary school were adequate but not exceptional, causing me to rank in the upper half or quarter of the class. Being the youngest and one of the smallest boys in class (the age gap eventually widened to two years because most of my classmates had to repeat a grade at one time or another), I did poorly in gym and hated it. That problem was aggravated by klutziness; I did no better outside school when trying to learn skating and swimming. Other weak subjects were drawing and singing, owing to complete lack of talent. I was bookish and aloof, and never had more than two close friends. Erica was indignant when she discovered on a few occasions that my best friend was the son of a worker or fisherman, but her attempts to steer me toward higher-class friends failed. *"You can lead a horse to the water…"*

I also was a show-off and was threatened with expulsion more than once for misdeeds such as walking up stairs on the outside of the banister, or darting out in front of cars. Another problem was my short temper. As my first homeroom teacher sweetly reminded me at graduation 7 years later, I had once threatened to unleash the entire Baltic Sea on her.

A crucial turning point in my development came around age 8. Among my father's books, I discovered a German 1000-page world history, which I read and re-read with growing fascination. From that book I acquired a gallery of heroes, from Achilles and Alexander the Great to King Gustavus Adolphus of Sweden. I was fascinated by the story that young Achilles was offered the choice between a short, glorious life with lasting fame or a peaceful, long life in obscurity. He chose the former, and I resolved to do likewise if a deity ever came to ask. I eventually realized that there really were 4 combinations rather than 2, but although no deity ever asked me, I am satisfied with the combination I got.

Next, my brother and I obtained two volumes of German youth magazines, which introduced me to astronomy, paleontology, and geology. My interest in chemistry awoke at about that time, and with the benefit of some 75 years' hindsight, it seems that the seeds for my later career in cosmochemistry were planted right then. My work on the origin of meteorites has enabled me to combine all four subjects that fascinated me by age 9: history, astronomy, geology, and chemistry.

We joined a Jewish Boy Scout troop for a year but then dropped out, for lack of interest and/or money. Most of these boys attended Jewish schools, so we had little contact outside the Boy Scout activities.

Father apparently was looking for a new line of business in the early 1930s. The largest business in town (*Liepāja Wire Factory*, now *Liepājas Metalurgs*) went bankrupt in October 1932, and father bought for liquidation the department store that it had maintained for its workers. Although we scrupulously paid for all the bargains we bought for ourselves (tin soldiers, shoes, etc.), my father lost money on the deal. Then he opened a *Bata* shoe store in partnership with uncle Arthur. (The latter's Czechoslovakian background may have been helpful, as *Bata*, a manufacturer of low-priced shoes, was a Czech company). But the store was unprofitable, and closed a year or two later.

Father took a business trip to Berlin in 1935, but expressed neither then or later any alarm over what he had seen in Germany. Perhaps he simply hadn't seen much, but actually, there was a 2-year lull between the anti-Semitic persecutions of early 1933 and the Nuremberg Laws of late 1935, and another lull until the 1936 Berlin Olympics; most German Jews were staying in Germany in the hope that the situation had stabilized. Hitler's first military move (into the Rhineland) was nearly a year away. Father brought us California apples as well as German toy soldiers, without any inkling what roles their places of origin would later play in our lives.

THE DEPRESSION HITS, 1936–1937

Our finances may have begun to tighten as early as 1933, when we moved into another apartment of the same size but in a less posh building on Peldu (Bade) St. 33. Things must have gotten quite a bit worse by the end of 1935, when we gave up our maid and governess and moved into a tiny 4-room attic apartment (about 45 m^2 ≈ 500 ft.^{2}) in my grandmother's house at Toma (Thomas) St. 56. It had low, sloping ceilings, a tiny kitchen with a sink, but no bathroom and only an unheated non-flush toilet in the hall. Access was by a steep, narrow staircase, and the ambiance was so shabby that we never let anyone visit us there. Visitors were received in grandmother's living room.

The only household help we could still afford (for a few months) was a middle-aged cleaning woman who came once a week. She was said to drink denatured alcohol with her boyfriend. Perhaps the pyridine in this beverage had dulled her sense of smell, but whatever the reason, she rarely bathed or changed her underwear. I made myself a paper gas mask and put it on whenever I had to walk through the room where she was. Lacking a charcoal filter, it was only of symbolic value, of course.

Father's export business had dried up during the Depression. The grain mill still operated but was not very profitable, and its meager income had to be shared with two partners and Grandmother Henna, who, with Father, had inherited Grandpa Israel's share. The household money left for Erica was very inadequate. Cod, the cheapest fish, appeared often enough on our table to last me for a lifetime. Our daily food budget often amounted to a very skimpy Ls 1.00 = $0.20 (comparisons for different times and countries are difficult, but that was equal to 1 hour of a teacher's pay, or the price of 3 lbs of sugar, or postage for 5 domestic letters). Moreover, my parents had to keep up appearances, dressing and acting as if business was still going well. We skimped wherever we could; for school, we bought second-hand books that often were one edition behind those used by the class, leading to occasional social and academic embarrassments.

Soon after we had moved into this palace, my parents had a fierce clash, rating 7 or 8 on the Richter scale. Erica discovered that my father had a mistress!

What brought on the earthquake was a silver-backed pocket mirror with an engraved dedication, which Erica had found in Father's pocket. She smashed it in extreme fury, packed her suitcase, and went to Rīga, where she stayed with her best friend Ella. A couple of months later she came back, presumably having worked out a truce with the help of friends and relatives.

Father gradually took more interest in me and my schoolwork. He designated an armchair as the "multiplication chair" and whenever I sat down in it, he quizzed me on the multiplication tables, forward and backward. The hardest was 7×8. When I got an F in a geography test, he proceeded to teach me better study habits (note-taking, outlining, etc.). My grades recovered.

One advantage of living in Grandma's house was her large garden. It had fruit trees, berry bushes, and flowers as well as an arbor and a pavilion, but had been totally neglected for years. At age 10, having learned in science class about chemical fertilizers, I decided to reclaim a few square feet of wilderness to grow some vegetables. My first crop of radishes and spinach succeeded splendidly, even though I naively gave each of them only the one kind of fertilizer that was needed for the edible parts: potassium for roots or nitrate for leaves. My parents even paid me for my crops, so with Father's help, I set up double-entry bookkeeping for expenses and income. That's as close as I ever came to becoming a farmer or businessman. Alas, although I had read about tenant farmers in my history book, it had not occurred to me to give part of my crop to Grandma Henna. She reprimanded me in no uncertain terms.

With the export business in the doldrums, Father put all his energies into the mill, and found it to be inefficient and poorly managed. His two partners were of little help, but Father made steady progress in improving matters. As he became more familiar with the operation, he began to suspect systematic theft, most likely by the manager. But before he had a chance to get to the root of the matter, the government nationalized the mill in 1938.

Latvia had become a nationalistic dictatorship on 15 May 1934 after a coup by prime minister Kārlis Ulmanis, who now began to nationalize certain industries. (Unlike the Communist government 3 years later, the Ulmanis government *paid* the owner—perhaps a bit below fair-market value but in hard, exportable currency.) Although the regime was quite oppressive—it outlawed all political parties, jailed opposition politicians, and closed 95% of the press—it was not particularly anti-Semitic, patterning itself more on Mussolini than on Hitler. (Indeed, anti-Semitic organizations such as *Pērkonkrusts* and their literature were banned, Ulmanis made his personal friend, the Hasidic M.P. Mordecai Dubin, adviser on Jewish affairs, and Latvia until its final days continued to admit Jewish refugees from Germany, unlike most other countries). The nationalization program was aimed at specific branches, not specific minorities, so if Jews were overrepresented in those branches, the burden fell mainly on them. But Jews in other branches were left alone, and Jews were free to start new businesses in such branches.

THREE GOOD YEARS, 1937–1940

Business had picked up by 1937, enabling us in April 1937 to move from grandmother's attic into a 6-room apartment at Ulich St. 68. The new apartment was more modest than our first two, but still a huge improvement over the attic. We referred to this move by the biblical term "exodus from Egypt", which well expressed our feelings.

Together with a partner (Jakob Epstein), Father leased 5 of the 6 movie theaters in town. This business was more profitable than his previous ones, and also enabled me to see lots of movies for free, including those that—by the prudish standards of the time—were forbidden to children under 16. Movie reels lasted only half an hour, so every half hour the lights went on for the projectionist to change reels and occasionally also the carbon electrodes of the arc lamp. During these breaks, any teachers in the theater scanned the audience looking for their pupils, but the ushers thoughtfully seated us in boxes in the rear, where we could duck whenever the lights came on. We saw many good movies as well as American cartoons during those months. One of my favorites that I saw several times was "San Francisco" (starring Clark Gable and Jeanette Macdonald), with great scenes of the 1906 earthquake. Little did I know that I would eventually end up in the area.

Father also resumed grandfather's grain export business, now that the world was beginning to emerge from the depths of the Depression. He borrowed some money from his mother and uncle, renovated his warehouse, and set up an office there. Sales soon picked up, and he quit the movie partnership in order to concentrate on his export business. At one point an interesting business opportunity seems to have arisen in Southern France, and for several weeks my parents talked seriously about a move. Nothing came of it, and by hindsight, it would have made little difference, as foreign Jews in France were summarily deported to Auschwitz in 1942/43.

6. The family, July 1939.

These were wonderfully carefree years. After years of extreme austerity, our living standard rose steeply. We bought furniture, clothes, dishes, a big radio, etc., and regularly enjoyed many small luxuries (by Liepāja standards of the 1930s) that we could not afford in "Egypt": pastries, ice cream, tropical fruit, and other delicacies. Although we still kept a kosher household with the required 4 sets of dishes and observed the major holidays, we occasionally partook in forbidden foods, such as pork, smoked eel, crayfish, etc. Father always took the initiative in such matters, being less religious than Erica who disgustedly referred to the crayfish as "queer worms", unconcerned about taxonomic accuracy.

Business kept improving and in 1939 father bought us fancy, chrome-plated bikes. We developed closer relationships with our parents, going for walks, chatting in the living room for hours in the evening, listening to the radio, doing crossword puzzles in German magazines, etc. Being self-employed, father took time off whenever he wanted to, and in the summer, we often went to the beach together, spending hours sunbathing, kayaking, etc.

During this happy period in July 1939 a visiting friend snapped a picture of each of us (Fig. 6). Blindly optimistic, none of us expected WWII to start in less than 2 months.

We continued to have meals together: dinner at 3 and supper at 7:30. Father would occasionally have a beer or a small glass of vodka, and we were then allowed to have some. Alcohol had never been forbidden fruit to us, as wine has a formal role at major Jewish holidays and is given even to children (we had our own, tiny silver goblets, from which we took a sip at the prescribed times.)

I was about 11 when my father taught me a lesson in honesty. We had become friends with Sigurd, the son of the Baltic German owner of our building, who showed us how to get some German youth magazines for free. A downtown store that carried these magazines returned the covers of unsold copies to the distributor for credit, but then sold these slightly mutilated magazines at a bargain price. Prospective buyers could look through the whole stack at leisure while the owner waited on other customers. Our friend taught us to slip a few magazines under a sweatshirt while the owner was not looking and then buy only one or two copies. We repeated the heist a couple more times but soon my father found out and made us return the stolen copies.

A few years later, in high school, Father taught me another ethics lesson. I had clashed with my English teacher for some silly reason (presumably I misbehaved, was reprimanded, and talked back), and now began to worry about the consequences. Father rightly concluded that I had been in the wrong and urged me to apologize. That was an unpleasant task, but I gave myself a push and apologized to the teacher. She graciously accepted the apology, and remained on very friendly terms with me thereafter. That lesson stuck with me all my life; I readily admitted error and greatly respected other people who did so.

The only thing that clouded our life were the frequent quarrels between my parents, over my father's mistress or other matters. Georg and I hated these ugly and noisy scenes, and during one particularly fierce clash, we jumped out of the window (a high first floor) and ran off to the park.

Early Teens

By age 12 I was interested in the adult world, and regularly read the German, Swiss, and Latvian weeklies we subscribed to. I also tried to help my father in his business, translating coded telegrams that came in his absence, or analyzing grain samples for purity. Only later did I realize that I was becoming his favorite. Once, after another clash with Erica, he asked me—not Georg—to take some papers to the bank for a major financial transaction. (Actually Erica decided to go with me, and insisted that *she* rather than this 12-year-old kid take the papers in).

Often I surfed the shortwave band on our radio, and became particularly interested in a couple of clandestine German stations that broadcast anti-Nazi news a few hours a week. One day I was listening to one of them when it suddenly went off the air in mid-sentence. It never came back. I began to realize what a police state was like but never thought that I soon would be living in one.

Having become interested in farming, I tended some chickens in our back yard. I avidly read books on poultry farming, and, eager to do everything right, bought numbered foot rings for my chickens, although I could easily tell the 3 of them apart. Alas, the chickens ate the poisoned bait I had laid out for rats, and all expired.

I had been a real bookworm for years, and had read hundreds of books from the school and city libraries. I worked my way through most of their holdings of popular science as well as Latvian translations of Jules Verne, Mark Twain, Jack London, Alexandre Dumas, Guy de Maupassant, Henryk Sienkewicz, Edgar Wallace, etc. I was especially intrigued by Verne's *Five Weeks in a Balloon*, where the hero's chemical knowledge enabled 5 latter-day Robinson Crusoes to attain 19th century living standards within a few years of landing on a desert island.

Traditionally, Latvia had been an agricultural country, and although it was steadily industrializing, farming was still glorified. Feeling very patriotic, I wanted to become an agronomist and planned to apply to the agricultural high school in Aizpute. Fortunately we had to take a battery of aptitude tests in the last year of elementary school. The counselor strongly dissuaded me from going into agriculture, but seeing that my logic score was 100 whereas my math score was (an inexplicably low) 12, he tried to steer me from my second choice, chemistry, to law. That had indeed been my ambition at age 6, when I asked my father how one could make the most money with the least amount of work, and he replied "as a lawyer". But now chemistry looked much more interesting.

High School, 1939–1941

Nonetheless, I was headed for a career in civil engineering after graduating from elementary school in 1939. My father felt strongly that a liberal *Gymnasium* education was of little value in a depressed economy. Though hoping that Georg and I would eventually attend university, he wanted us to have some marketable skills when we graduated from high school. He therefore sent us to the local all-boys' *Technicum*, which offered programs in mechanical, electrical, and civil engineering. (Such a school has no equivalent in the USA. It ranks somewhere between a technical high school and an engineering college). I understood that I could still switch to chemistry once I got to university.

I flunked the essay part of the entrance exam but was allowed to repeat it, having scored an A on the math part. Shattered, I took remedial lessons during the summer and passed. I was proud to have made it into high school and enjoyed wearing the required black uniform and blue/green school hat.

World War II broke out on 1 September 1939, just as I started high school. Smug in our neutral little country, we expected nothing worse than food shortages, and stocked up on staple foods. We did not know that Hitler had ceded the Baltics to the Soviet "sphere of influence" in a secret annex to the Hitler-Stalin pact of 23 Aug 1939. Indeed, a few weeks later the USSR forced the three Baltic countries to yield a number of military bases. Liepāja, having been one of the main naval ports of the Tsarist Empire, received a large Soviet garrison.

Though Soviet troops were now swarming through the streets of my hometown, and German troops were only 70 km away [since March, 1939, when Hitler had seized the Klaipėda (Memel) territory from Lithuania], we did not anticipate the coming danger and made no effort to emigrate. There were reasons, of course: most countries were not exactly vying for immigrants (especially Jews), my father was not sure whether he could support us in a new country, his export business was going well at last, and he did not want to abandon his mother and other elderly relatives. And the Soviet-German non-aggression pact of August 1939 seemed to assure peace in our corner of the world. When Hitler in October 1939 summoned Baltic Germans "home to the Reich", we misinterpreted this signal, thinking that now he would have no reason to invade the Baltic countries.

I enjoyed high school, worked harder, and to my complete surprise found myself at the top of the class. (While holding that rank for 2 years, my grade point average slowly crept up from B– to B+; an indication of bygone grading standards). My best friends were **Zigurds Fīlics** (1924–2003) and **Georg Spektor** (1925–1941), both shown in Fig. 7.

Zigurds' parents worked in the theater, the father as a stage hand and the mother in the costumes department. He was an only child, so when his parents were at work, he had the run of the apartment. The Spektor family was quite prosperous. They had Liepāja roots but had lived in Germany for decades and returned to Liepāja in ~1937/38. Georg was smart, worldly, well-educated, and my chief competitor for top rank in class. Georg's older brother, Eduard (~1923–1941), was my brother's classmate. Both perished in 1941.

7. *Georg Spektor (upper left), Zigurds Fīlics (lower left), myself (1939/40). The fourth boy mischievously held up 2 fingers to adorn me with horns.*

As in my elementary school, there was little anti-Semitism in high school. But once a big bully made some anti-Semitic remark to Georg Spektor, who spoke Latvian with an accent. I challenged the bully to a fight, to be held the next morning before class. Being two years younger than my classmates and one of the shortest, I borrowed a book on jiu-jitsu (similar to karate), not realizing that one does not learn this skill in one afternoon. I looked through the book and was impressed by the many ways to send one's opponent flying. Most of them started from a lying position, so I made the strategic decision to get onto my back as quickly as possible, and then flip my opponent. I spent the rest of the afternoon rehearsing these flips, and confidently headed to school the next morning half an hour early, where my classmates were already waiting for the spectacle.

We wrestled for a few seconds, and according to plan, I offered only token resistance when my opponent pushed me down on my back. However, I had neglected to define the rules, so as soon as I was on my back, my opponent was declared the winner. Actually, he was quite friendly to me from then on, and my other classmates also seemed to respect me more for defending my friend.

Yet there also were some fanatical anti-Semites in town. A *Gymnasium* student whom Zigurds knew resented the Soviet garrison (in 1939) even more than we did, and decided to set up a paramilitary resistance organization. He invited Zigurds to join who in turn nominated me. The founder decided that we should all have military ranks, and having appointed himself captain, he commissioned Zigurds and me as lieutenants. We were to wear Latvian officers' insignia on the underside of our school uniform collars. I went to one desultory meeting at the beach that was attended by about half a dozen co-conspirators, but a couple of weeks later Zigurds told me that there had been a second meeting, at which the Captain severely reprimanded him for bringing a Jew into the organization, tore off his insignia, and expelled him. Nothing ever came of this organization, as far as I know.

Dabbling in Chemistry

My interest in chemistry started at about age 9 on a very childish level, with a neatly labeled collection of chemicals from my parents' medicine cabinet, augmented by odd acquisitions such as a piece of zinc salvaged from the sink of our school's science lab, some manganese ore picked up on a plant visit, etc. In my packrat-like acquisitiveness, I also collected some empty ampoules and other glassware discarded by our neighbor dermatologist, who according to the custom of the time also treated VD patients. My mother was horrified by these latest showpieces, being sure they were infected with VD germs.

My chemical activities took an upswing in 5th grade when I became friends with my classmate, **Haralds Neimanis** (Fig. 8). Not only did his mother work at a pharmacy, which gave us access to many chemicals, but also his parents were seldom home and very tolerant (as Haralds, an only child, had a heart condition). We turned his apartment into a laboratory, using a chandelier as a source of glass tubing, and filling the house with vile smells from burning sulfur and other chemicals.

8. Haralds Neimanis (1938). He probably came to a sad end in WWII.

My chemistry projects at that time were always silly, and sometimes dangerous or illegal. I was fascinated by explosives, and played not only with acetylene-air mixtures but also with mixtures containing potassium chlorate. Fortunately, the explosion of a small sample deafened me for a few minutes, thereby teaching me to miniaturize such experiments. I also tried to convert denatured alcohol into drinking grade vodka by redistilling it over zinc chloride, but the product still stank so horribly of pyridine that I was in no danger of prosecution by the State Liquor Authority.

At age 13, a mild case of teenage secretiveness got me interested in invisible inks. Realizing that most of these inks were based on the color tests of qualitative analysis, I looked up W. D. Treadwell's university textbook on this subject, and became sufficiently interested to read it from cover to cover. Another good though ancient book that exposed me to classical inorganic chemistry was a *ca.* 1905 edition of Hollemann's *Inorganic Chemistry*. Looking back at this period, I think that the large amount of descriptive chemistry picked up at that time was very useful to me at later stages of my career.

Those Baltic Germans who obeyed the Führer's call in October 1939 sold their surplus belongings before departure. That's how I acquired a collection of chemicals and a few more chemistry books. As my chemical horizons widened my wish list grew. I had acquired a number of relatively common, safe chemicals, but now had my eyes set on others that were either rare or dangerous. I contrived, with my similarly inclined friend Zigurds Fīlics, to persuade our chemistry teacher to let us help him reorganize his rather chaotic chemicals cabinet. We met in the school lab for a few evenings consolidating and labeling bottles, and whenever our teacher left the room, we whipped out little envelopes and helped ourselves to chemicals we coveted.

That was not a feasible approach for metallic sodium, which is flammable in air and must be stored under kerosene. I therefore put some kerosene into a glass-stoppered bottle, wrote "Sodium" on the label, soiled it to simulate wear, and then one cold morning ran without an overcoat to a nearby pharmacy, panting: "We have just run out of sodium in the *Technicum* chemistry lab; could you please give me 20 grams?" The gullible pharmacist complied.

We did not do so well with nitric acid. Having obtained concentrated sulfuric acid from a trusting salesman, we wanted to add it to saltpeter and distill off the nitric acid formed. While Zigurd's parents were at work, we set up the experiment in his attic locker, using an alcohol lamp as the heat source. We assembled a retort and a receiver, but fearing that some nitric acid vapors might escape, we joined the vessels with a tightly fitting stopper—ignorant of the basic rule, *Never heat a closed system!* Watching the distillation from a peephole, we were pleased to see vapors rise in the retort, but as the air expanded on heating, pressure built up and the apparatus came apart with a loud pop. Stupidly, we tried it again, with exactly the same result.

4. SOVIET OCCUPATION: 1940/41

LATVIA BECOMES A SOVIET COLONY

THE FIRST OF several disasters struck on June 17, 1940. While Germany was crushing France, the USSR presented ultimatums to the 3 Baltic countries, demanding that they dismiss their cabinets and let the Red Army occupy the countries in their entirety. The excuses offered were wonderfully clumsy. Latvia and Lithuania (combined population 5 million) allegedly had a secret treaty to attack the Soviet Union (population 180 million). Estonia (population 1.1 million) was not charged with being a party to this conspiracy, but had apparently earned retribution for some other misdeeds at precisely the same moment. Two days earlier the Soviets had attacked 3 Latvian border posts, killing 3 guards and the wife and son of one of them. But they brazenly claimed that the Latvians had attacked first.

The governments had no choice but to give in. Soviet troops fanned out from their bases in the Baltic countries and linked up with other units that had crossed the borders. The Soviets forced the heads of state to appoint puppet regimes and then quietly arrested the previous cabinet. Most were dead a year later.

My father's bank accounts were frozen immediately and the press began a hate campaign against capitalists, using buzzwords such as bourgeois, exploiters, bloodsuckers, plutocrats, etc. Now it was clear that we should have left Latvia, but it was too late—the Soviets had sealed the borders. Our last chance was the Swedish freighter *Signfred* that happened to be in port on 17 June, loading a cargo of oats that my father had sold to Sweden. We briefly wondered if the captain might be willing to take us on as stowaways, but as the piers were heavily guarded by Soviet soldiers, we didn't even bother to ask. The ship left a few days later.

Soon the Sovietization of the country began under the direction of Andrei Vyshinsky, chief prosecutor at the notorious Moscow show trials of the 1930's. Yesterday's heroes—the founders and government of independent Latvia—became villains, and vice versa. There was wholesale rewriting of history; kings and emperors were "out" (except for Peter the Great, who had made Russia strong), and so were Old Bolsheviks like Trotsky, Zinoviev, Kamenev, Bukharin, etc., who had been purged in 1937. But various obscure revolutionaries were "in", all the way back to Spartacus, the leader of a slave revolt in ancient Rome. The Paris Commune of 1871 was celebrated as one of the most glorious high points of world history. The quartet Marx-Engels-Lenin-Stalin (preferably pronounced in one breath) was Communism's answer to the Holy Trinity, and Felix Dzerzhinsky, founder of the dreaded *Cheka* (secret police) had the status of at least a saint in this new religion.

In mid-July, a sham election was held, with a single "Communist and Non-Partisan" slate. A few naive patriots who had organized new parties and filed candidate slates promptly vanished, and their slates never appeared on the ballot. The resulting "parliament" at once proclaimed Latvia an independent *Soviet* republic. Its next act was to petition the Supreme Soviet of the USSR to admit this lone republic into the happy Union of Soviet Socialist Republics. After several days of suspense, the Supreme Soviet graciously acceded to this request and admitted Latvia as the 15th Soviet republic. Curiously, the

will of the people had worked exactly the same way in
Lithuania, Estonia, and Moldavia, and these republics also made
it into the Soviet Union within a day or two of Latvia. Many
years later a Soviet military map printed in 1939 came to light,
showing the Baltic States as part of the USSR. One cannot help
but marvel at such clairvoyance.

Liepāja had a reputation of being a "red" city, and indeed, on
my 1940 summer job with a cabinetmaker, I found that a number
of workers were pleased with the change. They believed the lofty
communist slogan: "From each according to his ability, to each
according to his needs", or more specific promises such as free
education and free medical care. Many of them had grudges
against the rich (no wonder, considering how some of us had
treated them!), and expected Stalin, like a latter-day Robin Hood,
to take from the rich and give to the poor. But when I met one of
these workers some 8 months later, he was bitterly disappointed.

The workers' anger was also directed against the police. A
young rookie policeman in our building, who had obtained his
new uniform only a few days before the Soviet takeover, was
beaten up by a mob of workers. Soon the police were renamed
"People's Militia". Many policemen were replaced by workers of
reliable proletarian background. A workers' paradise apparently
needs more police than a country enslaved by capitalists, so the
militia and their allies, the NKVD,[6] took over two of the largest
apartment buildings in town. Thoughtfully, the basement level
windows were immediately bricked in, to permit torture and
executions without disturbing the neighborhood. People began
to watch what they said and to fear the doorbell. That fear was to
stay with us the next 5 years.

PAUPERIZATION, MIND CONTROL

Nationalizations began in August, when all securities,
mortgages, etc. had to be surrendered. Then, at 11 PM on
September 30, my father was summoned by phone to his office,
where four men informed him that his business was being

---

[6] This was the dreaded secret police, which changed its name every decade or
so: Cheka, GPU, NKVD, MVD, and finally KGB. They wore army uniforms
with deceptively cheerful sky-blue insignia and hats.

"nationalized" without compensation. (The proper term would be *confiscated*). However, my father was generously permitted to keep responsibility for his business *debts* (loans from his mother, uncle, etc.); the nationalization extended only to his *assets*. And he was retained as manager for a transition period at a modest salary. Next the confiscations were extended to smaller and smaller stores and businesses, down to one-man tailor, shoemaker, and barbershops. For a haircut, you no longer went to Mr. Rosenblum the barber, but to Barber Shop #21.

Buildings with a net living space larger than 220 m^2 (~2400 sq ft) also were confiscated, as were farms larger than 30 ha (75 acres). Lacking the manpower to survey all buildings in town, the government requisitioned for this job the better high school students (in our class, Georg Spektor and me), who could presumably afford to miss a few days of classes. Grandma Henna's house missed the cutoff by a hair, but she had to rent several rooms to a Russian officer and his family. Grandpa Aaron's apartment building was confiscated and his petition for reconsideration was rejected, although he was 83 and had no other source of income. The Nazis solved that problem a year later.

One item that was not in short supply was Soviet soldiers; the garrison was not much smaller than the civilian population. Needing housing for military officers, the government rationed each person's living space to 9 m^2, and required any excess to be rented. (This quota was generous; in the USSR it was 7 m^2). "Transit" rooms that tenants had to walk through did not count, so we managed to hang on to our living room by renting our study and my bedroom. The rental income, along with my mother's earnings from Russian lessons, supplemented my father's salary. We were lucky to get two Latvian roomers, but many families got Soviets. Soon anecdotes circulated in town about naive Russians who were ignorant of Western plumbing, sanitation, and manners. A major's family in our building used newspapers for a tablecloth and conversed in wonderfully earthy language, and some other officers' wives proudly appeared at the opera in long, lacy nightgowns that they had bought in local stores. The government quietly campaigned against all such "uncultured" (*nyekul'turno*) behavior, but the path from diagnosis to cure was long.

About 4 months into the occupation, people suddenly lost most of their cash when Latvian money was declared void overnight, leaving Soviet rubles as the only currency. There was no possibility of exchanging Latvian money for rubles, so until next payday, most people had only those few Soviet bills that they had received as change when both currencies were in circulation. Everybody was poor now. (We had hoarded a few dozen Latvian silver coins, which came in handy 4 years later.) In a display of skillful "news management", the notice canceling Latvian money was a 1 column-inch item on the last page of the newspaper.

Latvia and the USSR had both been devastated by WWI and the subsequent fighting. But Latvia (without foreign aid!) had become prosperous by 1940, whereas the USSR, under horrendous communist mismanagement, remained dirt-poor in spite of her abundant natural resources. Now that Latvia had become their colony, the Soviets avidly bought up consumer goods from local stores that were scarce in the USSR, which meant everything, especially leather goods. (Meat was scarce in the USSR, and consequently so was leather.) Before store shelves were completely emptied, the government "equalized" prices to Soviet levels, which involved 10–30-fold increases for clothing and shoes. Wages were only doubled. I remember a man looking at the newly posted prices in a store window and laughing incredulously.

Some people undoubtedly gained from the Soviet occupation, such as communists, managers of nationalized property, etc. One fine example was streetcar conductor Jēkabs Sprūde. Though having only a 4th-grade education, he became a judge of the Liepāja District Court. But many others lost, if not individually then collectively, as prosperous Latvia was being dragged down to the level of poor USSR. To mitigate such discontent, the government occasionally gave Latvia a sop, such as shipment of a million tangerines. But mainly it relied on clumsy, cynical, and brazen *"Agitprop"* (agitation and propaganda; both were clean rather than dirty words in the communist vocabulary). Every day, the media compared our glorious life under Comrade Stalin with our miserable past in independent Latvia, although everybody knew how much our living standard had fallen and our freedom had eroded. We only had to look at the shabby Soviet soldiers whose overcoats frayed at the bottom for lack of a seam, the uncouth officers who invaded our stores like locusts, or the army trucks that popped like firecrackers owing to the low octane rating of their fuel.

In school, we had *Agitprop* as a new subject, covering Stalin's 1937 constitution and other marvels of this most perfect system ever invented by man. There were patriotic Russian songs to match, with lines such as "I know no other country where man breathes so freely". English was dropped as a foreign language and replaced by Russian. Previously unknown Soviet authors dominated the bookstores, magazines, and curricula. The most heavily promoted book was "And Quiet Flows the Don", a Russian civil war novel by Stalin's favorite author and later Nobel Laureate Mikhail Sholokhov. My classmates soon found a gang rape scene in that book, but lost interest when the rest turned out to be tamer.

The Soviets also put their stamp on industry. Ambitious production goals were set by the (5-year) *plan*, with each worker responsible for a *norm*. But workers were driven hard to exceed the norm. The most eager beaver in each factory was celebrated as a "Stakhanovite" (after Soviet coal miner A. G. Stakhanov, who had exceeded the norm 14-fold), but then the norm for everybody was raised substantially, if not always to the Stakhanovite's level. Quality was sacrificed to quantity; so for example, the men who crated window glass produced many more crates, but with much of the glass broken by hastily hammered nails. For some products such as nails the norm was specified by weight regardless of size, so small nails became scarce whereas big ones were plentiful.

Most of my classmates were unhappy about Latvia's loss of independence; only one was an enthusiastic communist who later became a celebrated terrorist.[7] We paid lip service to the

---

[7] That was Imants Sudmalis, b. 1916 and thus some 8 years older than most of us. He was active in the communist underground from about age 16, but was

system, but secretly ridiculed it. I lived in chronic fear that our *Agitprop* teacher would discover an anti-Soviet cartoon that a teacher had confiscated from me a few months before the Soviet takeover and presumably placed in my file. This cartoon, from the Swiss weekly *Weltwoche*, showed Stalin angrily berating two generals for their poor performance during the Russo-Finnish war of 1939/40. They defended themselves with the words "But comrade Stalin, we were outnumbered: three Finnish battalions against two of our divisions!"

Fortunately nobody in my school tried any organized opposition, nor did the "Captain" who in 1939 expelled Zigurds and me from his underground organization. In the Jelgava *Technicum*, a dozen seniors formed a resistance cell, organized similar cells in other schools, and posted hundreds of leaflets all over town. The NKVD infiltrated the organization and soon arrested all members. Most were never seen again.

On every (communist) holiday, there were staged mass demonstrations, with compulsory attendance from schools, offices, and factories. We marched through town, past buildings decorated with giant paintings of the Politburo greats, to an open field where we stood for a couple of hours listening to *Agitprop*. May 1 wasn't so bad, but on the November 7 anniversary of the October Revolution it was quite cold.

Early in 1941 Hitler issued a second call to Baltic Germans to "come home to the Reich". With life in Soviet Latvia becoming ever more bleak and oppressive, even those who had ignored his 1939 call (like our Rīga friends Ella and Kolya Woita) now felt that Nazi Germany was the lesser evil, and left. With tacit Soviet consent, the definition of "German" was broadened to include Latvians who feared persecution (former army and police officers, government officials, as well as Nazi sympathizers).

---

caught, spent 1933–36 in prison, and was rearrested in early 1940. A prominent member of the Communist Youth during Soviet rule, he kept a low profile during the German occupation, but had an accomplice plant a bomb in a public square in Rīga that was to explode during a mass meeting. It blew up prematurely, killing only 3 passersby. Both bombers were soon arrested by the German Security Police and were hanged in 1944. Despite the failure of the bomb plot, Sudmalis was virtually canonized by the USSR (Wikipedia).

DEPORTATIONS

They had gotten out just in time. On the morning of 14 June 1941 we discovered that quite a few families had been rounded up during the night and deported to Russia in freight cars. There was no clear pattern to the arrests: though many deportees were "capitalists" or other members of the upper and upper middle classes, others were teachers, farmers, shopkeepers or even workers of impeccable proletarian credentials. Perhaps the seeming randomness was a deliberate application of Stalin's principle that terror should be blind and arbitrary, so that no one feels safe. All together, 559 people, including 207 Jews, were deported from Liepāja, and ~15,000 from the whole of Latvia. Deportations continued for the next 3 days and nights, as trucks carted people from their homes to the railway station.

We wondered when our turn would come, but a phone call at mid-morning on June 14 told us to pack one suitcase apiece and wait to be picked up. We hastily threw things into 4 suitcases, but realizing that we might be separated, we repacked accordingly.

As luck would have it, one of our roomers (Timoshenkov, a young ethnic Russian from Latgale) was a major in the Border Guards, the paramilitary unit helping the NKVD with deportations. When he first moved into our apartment, he wore civilian clothes, but then one day frightened my mother by appearing in full military regalia. He was out the entire first night of the deportations, but when he came home for a brief nap, my mother asked whether he could get us off the list. After some joking and teasing he agreed, and so the truck never came for us.

That probably was a good thing, because only 60% of the 15,000 deportees and arrestees survived the war. Father, like most other men, would have been classified as an arrestee and put in the Gulag, which few survived; Mother and we boys would have been exiled for life to some remote, primitive village in Siberia or another inhospitable part of the Great Fatherland. By 1942 Georg and I would have been drafted into the Red Army, thus getting a belated opportunity to atone for our draft-dodging ancestors of 1812 and our "bourgeois" background.

5. GERMAN RULE: DEADLY 1941

WAR!

SURPRISE AWAITED us Sunday morning, 22 June 1941: Germany had attacked the Soviet Union! Now I realized why I had to work until 7 PM the previous day—my birthday—on my summer job as junior draftsman at the City Architect's office, tracing and copying plans for air-raid shelter trenches. (This is an interesting point in view of the frequent claim that Stalin was completely taken by surprise by Hitler's attack, having discounted all advance warnings that 3.5 million German soldiers were massing at the border. The low-level officials in remote Liepāja would not have started a crash program on air raid shelters without firm orders from higher levels. I later learned that marshals Zhukov and Timoshenko got wind a week before the attack, but, being unable to persuade Stalin, apparently took some preventive measures on their own).

Our sympathies in World War II had been squarely with the West. We listened to the BBC daily and were elated by the all-too-rare successes and saddened by the many reverses. Yet when Hitler attacked the Soviet Union, we rooted for the Germans as the lesser evil. Both my parents had lived under German occupation in World War I, and though they had heard of concentration camps and anti-Semitism in Hitler's Germany, they trusted German civilization and expected nothing worse than physical labor and loss of some civil rights. Our German-Jewish friends, the Spektors—who had left Germany in 1937 or 1938—were equally optimistic. Indeed, the Nazis in their first few years had been less severe with Jews "of merit", such as those who had fought in the German army in WWI. My father naively hoped for better treatment, as he had a good reputation with his German customers, and had received a very appreciative letter from one of them for warning him of a price-gouging attempt.

We did not know how murderous the Nazis had become. They had killed some tens of thousands of Poles and Jews in Poland in 1939/40, but we had not heard of these killings from either the local press—which wanted to keep good relations with Germany—or the BBC and the Swiss weekly *Weltwoche*. Anyhow, the "Final Solution" involving millions had not yet begun. What we knew was bad enough and should have made us worry, but we were all so sickened by the Soviets' deceit, hypocrisy, sophistry, coercion, terror, and lies, that the Nazis seemed the lesser evil.

Not everybody felt this way. Perhaps 1,000 people, including ~300 Jews, fled Liepāja in the first few days of the war before the city was cut off. Some were communists or collaborators whose lives had improved under the Soviets, some were blue-collar families that wanted to get away from the fighting, or, in the case of Jews, feared persecution by the Nazis. More might have fled but men—except party and government officials—were not allowed to leave.

The Germans advanced everywhere at amazing speed. But they ran into stiff resistance at Liepāja from Red Army troops and some 1000 volunteer "Workers' Guards". Dive bombers (an eerie sight, like a kamikaze changing his mind at the last moment) attacked the city at all hours, so from the second night on, we and ~40 neighbors slept in the basement of the building next door, staying there much of the day as well.

The Soviets were "afraid of their own shadow", as my father put it. They would shoot anybody standing on the roof, claiming that they were signaling German planes. Apparently it had never occurred to them how grossly impractical and unnecessary such a signaling method would be. They also killed the director and the boiler operator of the City Hospital (both Jewish), claiming that they had kept the boiler going to send smoke signals to German troops 4 km away, on the far shore of Lake Liepāja. In another incident, a Soviet patrol searched a man on the street and got suspicious about a steel tape measure in his pocket. When he started to open it to show what it was, they shot him on the spot.

On about the third day of the war, when we had emerged from the basement during a brief lull between air raids, our doorbell suddenly rang frantically. We froze in position but rushed to the window when the ringing stopped and a motorcycle started up. It was "our" major Timoshenkov. He had moved out of our apartment at the start of the war and had no reason to return except perhaps to offer us passage to Russia. I have no regrets about missing this opportunity. Even if we, tainted as "capitalists", had somehow avoided the Gulag, we would have become cannon fodder in the Red Army.

JEWS BECOME FAIR GAME

German troops captured Liepāja on 29 June, one week after the start of the war. Much of the center of town was destroyed by dive-bombers and especially by land and naval artillery fire during the final night, but we personally did not suffer. There were bomb craters in the streets, burned-out buildings, and much broken glass. The warehouses along the harbor had burned down, and the stench of burned grain hung over the city for days.

Our very first impressions of the Germans were favorable. We welcomed the signs "Looters will be shot" that went up everywhere, and my father noted approvingly how calm and self-assured the German soldiers were in contrast to the paranoid Soviets.

Within hours things became harsh. Unbeknownst to us, Hitler had decided in early 1941 to kill all Jews in the USSR during the planned invasion.[8] This was to be done by shooting. The decision also to kill West European Jews came nearly a year later during the Wannsee Conference of 20 Jan 1942. By then nearly a million Jews had been shot, including most of the Jews in the Baltic countries. But as the shooting proved to be stressful for some executioners and not fast enough, gas chambers henceforth were to be the preferred, more efficient method.

For the USSR the Nazis had organized the *SS-Einsatzgruppen*, 4 teams of about 600–900 men trained specifically for the "Final Solution". They followed hard on the heels of the Army, with orders to organize pogroms and executions, staging them so that they would seem to be spontaneous revenge actions by natives enraged at their "Jewish Bolshevik oppressors". *Einsatzgruppe A* under SS-*Brigadeführer* Dr. Walter Stahlecker was assigned to the Baltics, and one of its teams, *Einsatzkommando 1a*, arrived in Liepāja on the first day of the occupation. It promptly shot a few Jews and organized a Latvian volunteer "Self-Defense" force to root out communists and serve as auxiliary police, replacing the vanished Soviet police ("People's Militia"). Dozens of Jews and communists were arrested in the first few days and soon shot, but there was no sign yet of the impending Holocaust. On July 1, signs went up announcing that 10 hostages would be killed for any act of robbery or sabotage, and a week later the quota was raised to 100 hostages for every German soldier killed or wounded.

On 5 July the city commandant, *Korvettenkapitän* (navy major) Brückner, announced a set of anti-Jewish rules:

1. All Jews must wear an easily recognizable yellow marking of no less than 10 cm × 10 cm on their chest and back
2. All men from 16 to 60 must report for work daily at 7 AM at the Fire Station
3. The shopping time for Jews is 10–12
4. Jews are allowed to leave their quarters only 10–12 and 3–5
5. Jews are forbidden to attend public parks and the beach
6. When meeting a uniformed German, Jews must leave the sidewalk

---

[8] Ian Kershaw, *Fateful Choices: Ten Decisions That Changed the World 1940–1941.* New York: Penguin (2007), 431–470.

7. Jews are forbidden to use public transportation
8. Jewish shops must have a sign *Jewish Business* in the window,
   with letters at least 20 cm in size
9. Jews must turn in all radios, means of transportation, uniforms,
   weapons, and typewriters....
...11. Jews disobeying these orders will be treated with utmost
   severity.

Thus marked with yellow badges, Jews were often picked off the street by German military trucks and taken away. Soon eyewitnesses reported what had become of these people: they had been shot on the dunes near the fishermen's wharf (Fig. 9).

9. Jews digging their graves on Liepāja dunes. SD executioners on left; German soldiers in background, watching. (Early July, 1941)

Changing our Identity

In this grim situation, father thought up a plan that might save at least three of us, by taking advantage of our "Aryan" looks (we were blue-eyed and blond, except for Erica who was a brunette). Erica was to pretend that she was not the actual child of her Jewish parents, but a foundling discovered on their doorstep with a note bearing only her first name and a cross, indicating that she was Christian. Under the Nuremberg laws, this would make Georg and me half-Jews, and hence merely second-class citizens rather than total outcasts.

Had we known that the war would last another 4 years, we never would have had the courage to try my father's plan. Too many people in our small town could prove that the story was a lie. A woman was still living who had given birth to a daughter on the very same day Erica was born, in the same maternity ward. She surely knew that Erica was her parents' own child, not a foundling. Many other people had known Erica's two older sisters (deceased in 1927 and 1930), and realized that she looked too much like them to be a foundling. As it turned out, *the people who knew didn't want to hurt us and those who wanted to hurt us did not know.*

But we thought, with incredible naiveté, that the war might he over in less than a year, and figured our bluff might last that long. Luckily, in the 1930s my mother had been corresponding (in German) with the Rosicrucian Fellowship of Oceanside, California about her health and about family problems with her husband and mother-in-law. Apart from recipes for celery salad etc., they sent her good, common sense advice about turning the other cheek and trusting in Jesus Christ. The latter reference would now help to prove her Christian orientation.

After rehearsing the foundling tale, Erica and Georg went to the SD (= *Sicherheitsdienst,* a branch of the SS charged with security police functions as well as anti-Jewish programs in the occupied territories). Aided by her good looks, charm, imposing bearing, and histrionic talent, she persuaded the just-arrived SD-chief, *Untersturmführer* (lieutenant) Wolfgang Kügler, to issue passes to the three of us, stating that we were exempt from the laws and regulations affecting Jews. Obviously impressed by her, Kügler remarked with chagrin: "Jews always got the best German women". On leaving, Erica reciprocated with the *Heil Hitler* salute.[9]

Anxious to lower our profile, we decided to get rid of our shiny bicycles, although as half-Jews, we were technically permitted to keep them. We sold them to neighbors, and as we wheeled them out, we saw Father crying—for the first time since his father's death. Replying to Erica's question, he said: "I wanted to give some pleasure to the children, and now it is taken away".

Unfortunately my father's plan offered no protection to him. Like most members of his side of the family, he looked Jewish,

---

[9] Fortunately my mother did not know that Kügler was firmly committed to the Final Solution, and was to oversee it in Liepāja. In 1943 he spent 8 months in prison for appropriating Jewish property. In the upside-down world of the Third Reich, killing Jews was no crime, but stealing their property was.

even more so since he had broken his nose in his youth. But now help came from a Latvian friend, **Herta Kārkliņš** (Fig. 10). She was most anxious to help and found him a job as an unpaid farmhand, in the hope that the remoteness of the farm and the essential nature of his job would offer him some protection.

10. Herta Kārkliņš (early 1930s)

Not being interested in adults, I knew Herta only superficially. But in 2000 I obtained some biographical information from Indra Rutkis Michalovskis in Olympia, WA—Herta's goddaughter and her cousin's daughter. Herta worked in a law office but also played leading roles in the local theater. She was well-read and multi-lingual; a charming, sophisticated lady.

Herta's mother also took big risks to help Jews. After the ghetto was established, she repeatedly took food to the Jews, dropping it off where they would find it. She always took her little granddaughter along so as to look less suspicious. Being tall and as thin as a rail, she could hide a fair amount of food under her coat.

In 1943 Herta married a war correspondent in the Latvian Legion, Jānis Burķevics (1909–1965). With several relatives, she fled to Germany in the fall of 1944 and found shelter in the „Warthegau" (Western Poland, annexed to Germany). The Soviet advance in January 1945 forced them to flee westward, but the trip—on flatcars—took 4 days in fierce cold. Her newborn daughter Gunta came down with meningitis, and for lack of medical care became permanently retarded. A few years later the family emigrated to the

US and settled in Tacoma, where Herta gave birth to a son, Juris. She died in early 1997, a year before I nominated her for „Righteous Among the Nations". I had lost contact with her in 1944 and did not even know that she was in the US.

Only gentiles could help us now that Jews had become outcasts, and among those we knew, Herta seemed to be the most compassionate. She provided invaluable help several months later.

Kügler's passes saved us from arrest and execution. We got them none too soon, as mass murders of Jewish men began in early July, culminating in a major manhunt 22–25 July during which 1,100 men were killed. The Navy Commandant of the town, *Fregattenkapitän* (Navy Lt. Colonel) Kawelmacher, like many Nazis, apparently believed Nazi propaganda that Jews were the mainstay of the Soviet regime and would be the organizers and hard core of a guerilla movement. Complaining that the local SD was killing Jewish men much too slowly, he therefore asked the Commanding Admiral of the Baltic to send 100 SS-men to Liepāja for "rapid solution of Jewish problem". Obligingly a detachment of the Arājs Commando came, shot, and left.[10]

The Latvian police quizzed us a few times upon denunciation by local zealots, but always released us after seeing our passes. Most Latvians ranged from neutral to compassionate (the latter included even some police officials), but a few percent were rabid anti-Semites who would have preferred to see us dead rather than alive. Erica had a particularly difficult time and avoided certain streets entirely. When she ran into anti-Semites, they either yelled at her or tormented her with questions such as: *Where is your husband? How come you are not wearing a yellow patch? You know that the Jews started the war (or killed our ministers and generals, or burned down our cities). What do you say to that?*

Georg and I both had summer jobs, he in a machine shop and I as junior draftsman in the City Architect's Office. Two of my classmates, including my best friend Zigurds, also worked there.

---

[10] A notorious Latvian SD unit of a few hundred men under Viktors Arājs, organized by the German Einsatzgruppe A immediately after the capture of Rīga on 1 Jul 1941. Their main task was to kill Jews and communists in Rīga and the provinces.

Our first assignment was to inspect the basement of the department store in town, where a number of people had sought refuge during the siege, thinking that it was especially solid. However, none of them survived, as the building was hit by shells or bombs and burned out. Among the charred bodies, my colleagues found some 20 fire-blackened Tsarist gold coins, which had outlasted their owner.

Georg and I were not allowed to continue school, and when our summer jobs ended, we found that nobody would hire us. We subsisted from sale or barter of our belongings, and sporadic earnings from my mother's German lessons. (Most of her students were scholarly, but one young woman was highly focused on a specialized vocabulary, such as the German words for "undress", "underpants", etc.).

In late August, the police required all residents to have their passports re-validated, the better to identify Jews and other undesirables. Erica had no trouble, especially since the Latvian police clerk was demonstratively courteous and sympathetic. But Georg and I had to clear another hurdle. To qualify as half-Jews, we were to produce a certificate from the Jewish Council that we had never belonged to the Jewish religion. The head of the 2-person Council declined, as both my brother and I were circumcised, had Bar-Mitzvah, and had attended the temple on major holidays. But the other member, the young lawyer Menash Kaganski (1908–1945), came up with an ingeniously evasive formulation: "Adolf Alperovitch, father of Georg and Eduard Alperovitch, did not belong to the Jewish congregation". That was true; my father had resigned from the congregation some years ago, probably for political rather than religious reasons. (Only in 1997 did I realize that this half-truth had saved my life. The *Reichskommissar für das Ostland* (Governor of "Ostland", an artificial entity comprising the Baltics and Byelorussia, had issued secret guidelines in the summer of 1941 according to which half- and quarter-Jews were to be classified as Jews if they "belong or formerly belonged" to the Jewish religious community.)

Father Goes Into Hiding

Father was able to stay on the farm until the end of harvest (October), after which the farmer had no further use for him. Now Father was required to apply for work at the Labor Office, but that would have been tantamount to suicide. He therefore decided to hide in our apartment. We set up a hiding place in the pantry behind a row of firewood. Each time the doorbell rang, he was to climb over the wood and hide behind it before we answered the door.

These were difficult weeks for him. He had to stay away from the windows, speak softly, and always be ready to rush into his hiding place. Erica's nerves were stretched to the breaking point, and she reacted by frequent noisy scenes, directed mainly at Adolf. He and I engaged in an odd bit of escapism, continuing to draft plans for our post-war dream house that I had started during the Soviet occupation.

The police had made 2 brief searches of our apartment while Adolf was still on the farm, but left when we presented Kügler's talisman and claimed not to know where Adolf was. One day in late November we weren't sure whether the doorbell had rung or not, and so Adolf neglected to take cover while Erica went to the door. It was a Latvian policeman (Jānis Sproģis), looking for Adolf. With the route to his hideout cut off, Adolf quickly hid in the bedroom wardrobe, while Erica, trying to mask the noises from the bedroom, hysterically shouted at the policeman to tell her where her husband was, because the police had arrested him off the street a week ago. The ruse worked; the policeman was sufficiently flustered not to notice the noises and to miss the wardrobe on his subsequent search of the apartment.

But it was to no avail. Unbeknownst to us, both the janitor (Mr. Hippe, a Germanized Latvian) and our next-door neighbor had heard Adolf's voice through the walls and floors, and at least one of them had reported him to the police. They must have heard him again.[11] On 2 December, as I came home at noon from another fruitless job search, I heard the sound of firewood

---

[11] Just before we fled from Liepāja to Germany on 15 Oct 44, Hippe came to my mother, kissed her hand, and begged forgiveness without explaining what for. A clear enough admission of guilt.

tumbling to the floor, a German yelling at my father, and my father replying "But I am no criminal". Ten policemen, including the German *Hauptwachtmeister* (Technical Sergeant) Lemke, had searched the apartment and were about to give up when Sproģis, who was with the party, had the idea of looking behind the firewood.

The police took both my parents away. Two days later Lemke returned with one of the Latvians and walked through the apartment, looking for souvenirs. He assured me that my parents would soon be released, took the radio along, and left. [In 1999, a friend found in the LVVA files two official reports by Lemke about my parents' arrest. Lemke wrote that a Latvian policeman, Šrāders, had recently seen Adolf on the street. But that was a complete lie; Adolf had not dared to leave the apartment since October when he returned from the farm. The Soviets later sentenced Šrāders to 15 years in the Gulag for some other misdeeds.]

December 2 happened to be Georg's first day at work, at the local branch of the Danzig construction firm A. Dehlert. When he came home that evening I told him the bad news, and we both felt that we now were orphans. Georg continued to go to work while I stayed home and tried to get a meal ready for him by evening. Although I had learned a few years earlier how to bake cakes, my cooking skills were grossly inadequate. Fortunately Herta Kārkliņš somehow learned of our predicament and brought us food almost every night.

Herta sat in our kitchen the evening of December 8, when the door opened and Erica walked in, looking ashen. She had been released (on condition that she never tell anyone what she had seen or heard) but was told that Adolf would be shot. Both women rushed off to one of Herta's friends who was on very good terms with one of the top German navy officers. Nothing came of it; I don't recall whether the officer didn't want to get involved with the SD or tried and got nowhere. Erica went to the jail the next morning and saw from a distance how several prisoners, one of whom resembled Adolf, were being put on a truck. By the time she got to see Kügler, he told her Adolf had

56   5. *German Rule: Deadly 1941*

already been shot.[12] Later we got written confirmation that my father had "died" on 9 Dec. I doubt if he knew that the US had entered the war the day before; this would have brightened his last moments. But another thought may have helped him face imminent death. A few weeks before his arrest he said to me: "Who knows, perhaps *real* life starts only in the hereafter".

Naturally, Father's death was a heavy blow, as we had become quite close in the last few years. But the pain was less overwhelming than after my brother's death 2 years later. I can only guess possible reasons: Father was older, his life in hiding had become untenable, mother, Georg, and a few of my other relatives were still living, our own lives were in a more precarious state, etc.

After the war, I tried to track down Jānis Sproġis, the policeman whose zeal led to the arrest of my father. Erica claimed to have seen him in the Stargard/Pomerania transient camp in October 1944, so he evidently had fled to Germany at about the same time as we did. In February 1949, shortly before coming to the US, I inquired at the Central Database of Latvian Refugees in Germany and learned that Sproġis—born 24 Oct 1912 and formerly living in Liepāja on Dzintaru St. 54—was now in the Würzburg, Bavaria DP camp. I promptly reported the case to the Bavarian Indemnity Office in Munich. Not having heard from them before my departure, I wrote them from the USA and learned that an indictment had been forwarded from the District Attorney's Office to the German Courts Branch, both under the Military Government of Bavaria. However, I never heard from them again and doubt if any action was taken, because I probably didn't have enough of a case against Sproġis. Though a number of Latvian policemen took part in mass executions of Jews, I have no direct evidence that Sproġis did. The strongest verifiable charge is excessive zeal in finding my father. Many war criminals successfully evaded more serious charges by claiming to have acted under orders or threats of punishment. It is unlikely that Sproġis could have been convicted on this charge, especially in 1949, when the government and public wanted to close the book on war crimes. Yet I sometimes wonder if I shouldn't have made greater efforts to avenge my father.

---

[12] Two brief, anonymous references appear in the biweekly Situation Report of the *SS- und Polizeistandortführer Libau* of 13 Dec 1941: "In 2 cases Jewish apartments were searched, resulting in the arrest of 3 Jews who were put in Central Prison....During the report period, 88 people were executed in Libau, namely 35 communists and 53 Jews." (*Records*, folder 22).

I resumed the search in 1978–83, after my children were grown. But Sproģis is a rather common Latvian name, and Jānis even more so. Although I got help from the Office of Special Investigations in Washington and Simon Wiesenthal in Vienna,[13] none of the several candidates in the US and Canada matched policeman Sproģis in birth date and place. The American Latvian Association had at least one Jånis Sproģis from Liepāja, but before disclosing his address they first needed to get his permission, which apparently never came. IRS and Social Security records are unavailable for such purposes.

Most of the remaining Jews of Liepāja were shot 6 days after Adolf, on 15–17 December. I recounted my own experiences in Ch. 1, but for a broader perspective, I present here some official accounts from German sources.

DEATH IN THE SAND DUNES

Ezergailis[14] reports further details of the executions, based mainly on the records of the 1968–1971 *Landgericht Hannover* trial of 9 perpetrators.[15]

The killing ground was 15 km north of the city, at a former Latvian army practice range in the dunes of Šķēde, about 1 km from the road. Latvian policemen, supervised by the SD, marched groups of Jews from the prison to a wooden barn, less than 100 m from the pit (3 m wide and 100 m long). The executions started at 8 AM, and were done alternately by a German unit, the Liepāja Latvian SD platoon, and a Latvian Schutzmannschaften [auxiliary police] team.

The Jews were taken from the barn as needed in 20-person groups, and were made to lie face down 40–50 m from the ditch. Groups of 10 were told to stand up and undress (except for children), first to their underwear and after being driven to the pit, completely. Bulvāns saw [SS-men] Karl-Emil Strott and Philip Krapp use a whip on those who did not go to the pit. The victims shrieked, whimpered, cried, and fell on their knees in front of the executioners to beg for their lives. They were lined up on the seaside of the pit, facing the sea. The 20-man execution squad lined up behind them on the other side of the pit and fired at the victims, two bullets for each.

---

[13] We visited Wiesenthal in his heavily protected Vienna office in October 1980. He was a remarkable man, striving for justice rather than revenge and able to recognize humane traits even in war criminals (see his book „The Sunflower").

[14] Ezergailis, *Holocaust* 293–294; shortened and slightly paraphrased here.

[15] *Strafurteil gegen Erhard Grauel, Erich Handke, Otto Reiche, Karl-Emil Strott, Gerhard Kuketta, Paul Fahrbach, Philip Krapp, Josef Michalsky, Georg Rosenstock* (Landgericht Hannover, 1968–71).

Blood occasionally spurted on the clothes of the killers. Children who could walk were treated like adults, but babies had to be held by their mothers above shoulder height, with one bullet each for mother and child. For the corpses that did not fall into the ditch, there was a "kicker" who rolled them in. After each volley a German SD-man stepped into the ditch to finish off any victims still showing signs of life.

After killing 10 sets of victims, the team was relieved by another; SD men Strott and Erich Handke took pictures. Around noon, a milk can of rum appeared. The guards and killers drank by dipping a glass into it. High Wehrmacht and Navy officers visited the site.

The clothes were piled up in heaps and taken away by German military trucks. The action lasted until dark (sunset was at 3:42 PM). Executions continued for the next 2 days, but there are no eyewitness reports.

Some details in this report differ from those in 12 pictures of the executions that were taken by SD-man Sobeck on 15 Dec 41 and were surreptitiously copied by David Zivcon, an audacious Jew working in the SD building. For the killing action of 15 Dec, Jews were held not in the barn but out in the open, where they undressed and waited to be led to the pit. Many young women had to strip naked, but most other victims only stripped to their underwear and kept it on when they were shot. The shrieking, whimpering, and crying may indeed have happened when those victims still in a state of denial first realized what was in store for them. But by the time Sobeck took the pictures, the Jews were preparing for execution with complete stoicism. Only one picture, of several naked women running a gantlet of Latvian police, shows one of them in a state of agitation and despair. The ditch was 8 m rather than 3 m wide at the top and at least 3 m deep, thus it seems unlikely that an SD-man "stepped into the ditch" to fire mercy shots. More likely he fired from above.

Three consecutive pictures showing the execution of a group including the Grinfeld family are in Figs. 11–13.

11. *A group of victims, including 5 children or youngsters, is headed for the ditch. The boy in the dark shirt is Ruben-Aron Grinfeld (15), followed by his mother, Ita-Beile (38) and sisters, Ester-Liebe (13) and Cilla (9, only her leg and skirt are visible). Presumably they had just spotted the firing squad and a group of victims off to the right, as Ruben winces and Ester has turned around and is reaching for her mother. The sea is visible in the upper right.*

12. *The same group, lined up at the ditch next to a pennant marking the place where they were to stand. Ruben Grinfeld is second or third from the right, next to his mother and sisters. Little Cilla is holding her mother's hand. A "kicker" is visible on the extreme right, pushing bodies into the ditch that were stuck on the ledge.*

13. *Ruben in the dark shirt lies on the ledge, but the kicker is coming. The pennant apparently stayed in place until the bodies had piled nearly to the top of the 3-meter-deep ditch, and was then moved to ensure efficient filling of the ditch. There exists a less sharp but less contrasty version of this picture, showing the beloved Baltic Sea in the background.*

I had heard rumors of some of these details back in 1941. But it is eerie to read such a graphic description 55 years later, telling how my relatives died and what was in store for me if the Danzig policeman had said "stay" instead of "go".

This slaughter was a big event for our small town, yet it rated only 9 words in the January 30, 1942 progress report of *Einsatzgruppe A* on the extermination of Baltic Jews, which I saw at the Nuremberg trials in 1948. According to that report (which I later saw again in the US National Archives), 2,350 Jews were executed in Liepāja in those two days.[16]

SS-Obersturmbannführer (Lt. Col.) Dr. Fritz Dietrich, *SS- und Polizeistandortführer Libau,* in his handwritten "War Diary" gives a noteworthy account of the principal events of those 3 days:

---

[16] Ezergailis, *Holocaust,* 293. He reports 2749 in Šķēde and 270 on the naval base. The former is the total given in the 3 Jan 42 situation report of the *SS und Polizeistandortführer Libau,* Dr. Dietrich, but it probably includes the 270 on the naval base. (*Records,* folder 22).

15.12.41.	1) On 15.12.41 a member of the Wehrmacht was fired on in the Naval Port by unknown assailants. 2) Start of Judenaktion. On this day, 270 were shot at the Libau beach, behind the Naval Port. 3) Arrest of 3 Wehrmacht members who had close relations to Jewish women.	Cold, light frost
16.12.41.	1) Continuation of Judenaktion. 2) Move of Libau concentration camp to Frauenburg. 3) Arrest of 26 members of communist organizations. 4) Seizure of 425 kg meat and 40 kg bacon by price control staff.	Frost
17.12.41.	1) Completion of Judenaktion. All together, 2749 Jews were shot. Courland thus is free of Jews, except for about 350 Jewish craftsmen who are needed for essential work.	Light frost

14. Liepāja SS- and Police Chief Fritz Dietrich, 1 Jun 1942, flanked by Mayor Blaus (right) and General Dankers (left)

Dietrich (Fig. 14) was mistaken about the number of Jews left. He had intended to issue 350 pink passes to craftsmen only, but the people implementing his order also exempted immediate families. Thus at year's end 1,050 of the original ~6,500 Jews still remained. Kügler allegedly said, "Half will be done away with and the other half will be put into a ghetto". But when the ghetto was established on 1 July 1942, 832 Jews entered it. About 200 survived the war. (Dietrich was hanged in the Landsberg/Bavaria prison in 1948, not for the murders in Liepāja but for the execution of 7 allied fliers in July-August 1944 while he was police chief of Saarbrücken. Kügler hanged himself in 1959 while awaiting trial in a West German prison. Strott became a hotel manager after the war but was finally tried in Hannover 1968–71 and sentenced to 7 years in prison. Erich Handke, the most brutal of the Liepāja SD men, also was tried in Hannover in about 1971 and was sentenced to 8 years but died after 8 months).

Though the Latvian SD platoon in Liepāja was now doing a major share of the killings and Latvian auxiliary police helped by rounding up victims, most people of Liepāja remained opposed. In his semi-monthly report of 3 Jan 1942, Dr. Dietrich complains:

"The execution of Jews carried out during the report period still is the talk of the town. Often the fate of the Jews is deplored, and thus far few positive voices have been heard in favor of the elimination of Jews. Among others, there is a rumor circulating that the execution has been filmed, so as to obtain [incriminating] material against the Latvian auxiliary police. This material is supposed to prove that the executions were done not by Germans but by Latvians."[17]

Ezergailis (l. cit., p. 305) cites an earlier example: "...on October 11, 1941, Liepāja *Gebietskomissar* Alnor wrote to *Generalkomissar* Drechsler that the killing of the Jews had created a general dismay in the city. The mayor of Liepāja, he wrote, who usually agrees with everything, came to him and reported the 'great dissatisfaction' in the city...."

The decency of this "silent majority" has been widely overlooked in later years. Instead many people judge the Latvian nation by the crimes of its henchmen, although the executioners and helpers numbered only about 3,000 (<1% of the adult male population), according to Ezergailis. I discuss this matter in more detail in Part II.

FATE OF OUR RELATIVES

The first Nazi victims from our family may have been *great-aunt and -uncle Johanna and Arkady Goron* (71 and ~71) in Kaunas/Lithuania. As prominent *bourgeois* they should have been deported to the USSR on 14 June 1941, but according to the Lithuanian Archives, they were not on the list. The Germans

---
[17] *Records*, folder 22.

captured Kaunas on 24 June 41 and the SD promptly instigated a pogrom by Lithuanians, in which 3,800 Jews were killed. Rich people like the Gorons were the most likely victims. If they escaped this pogrom, they surely were killed later in 1941.

Latvians were harder to incite according to the Einsatzgruppen report,[18] so that much of the killing initially was done by Germans. Men came first. *Cousin Alya Fränkel* (28) went to his job as a pianist in the Hotel St. Petersburg in Liepāja on the second day of the occupation (30 June), not knowing that a detail of *SD Einsatzkommando 1a* had just chosen it as its headquarters. Erica later heard that they shot him on the spot. *Cousin Fred* (28) resumed work at the *Korona* leather factory as soon as Liepāja had fallen, but within a few days some German henchmen appeared and asked all Jews to step forward. His Latvian workers urged him to stand back, but he didn't and was taken away to be shot. *Great-uncle Lyova Ginsburg* (70) was arrested in one of the July manhunts, and *great-aunt Keile Alperowitz* (66) was picked up in October while standing in line at the only grocery store where Jews were allowed to shop. *Grandpa Aaron Sheftelovitch-Meiran* (83) was arrested on Jewish New Year's day (9/23), when he defiantly stood at the window of his apartment and prayed, all synagogues having been razed.[19] *Grandma Jenny* (81) was spared at the time, having been put to work chopping mortar off bricks from bombed buildings. I saw her at work one day and am still saddened by the memory of this frail, petite lady doing hard labor.

Our last 4 surviving relatives in Liepāja—my *grandmothers Henna Alperowitz* (71) and *Jenny Sheftelovitch-Meiran* (81), *great-aunt Johanna Ginsburg* (62), and *great-uncle Wulf Alperowitz* (63)—were swept up in the December 15–17 *Aktion.* Their final hours were not pleasant.[20] Most victims had to spend

---

[18] However, on 4 July 1941, the newly recruited Arājs Commando herded a number of Rīga Jews into the Gogol Street synagogue and burned them alive, allegedly together with some 300 Lithuanian Jews who had fled to Rīga at the start of the war and had found refuge in the synagogue.

[19] The War Diary of the Liepāja SS- and Police Chief Fritz Dietrich has the following entry for 9/24: "Woman arrested in Naval Port area on suspicion of espionage. 37 Jews executed in Libau. Rainy weather."

[20] Ezergailis, *Holocaust,* 293, writes: "The victims were brought to the Women's Prison, where Jews of all ages were jammed into the courtyard. As reports tell

the night in the crowded prison yard, were marched rather than driven 11 km to the execution site, and many had to strip naked in the December cold before execution. Grandma Henna, like many Jews, had hidden her diamonds in the seam of her coat. They must have been a nice surprise for whoever acquired her coat.

Most of our Rīga relatives fared no better. *Uncle* **Arthur Felsenburg** (50) appears in a list of Central Prison prisoners and so may have been killed early. *Cousin* **Herbert Felsenburg** (14) may have been killed either in July when *aunt* **Ida** (37) wrote that he and Arthur were "in the countryside", or with Ida, in the 30 Nov and 8 Dec 41 Rumbula massacres. *Uncle* **Leo Sheftelovitch** (43) lasted the longest. He had been spared as an essential worker, worked in the Olaine peat bog in 1943, and was deported to Stutthof in late summer 1944. On 3 Nov he was sent to the Magdeburg-Polte satellite camp of Buchenwald but died there in January 1945. His wife **Harriet Sheftelovitch** (43) and their little daughters, *cousins* **Lili** (7) and **Hedwig** (3), presumably perished in the big Rumbula killings of November or December 1941, as even "essential" workers were deemed not to need luxuries such as a wife and children. Leo had named his two daughters after his dead sisters, not knowing that the girls' lives would be cut short even sooner.

Unbeknownst to us, *cousin* **Para** (who desires anonymity for herself and her family) had fled to the USSR with her husband at the start of the war. He was drafted into the Red Army and was killed in action, but Para and her daughter survived. Her father stayed behind and was killed at Rumbula, but her brother-in-law survived in the ghetto for a couple of years and was then hidden for more than a year until the Soviets recaptured Rīga on 13 Oct 44. As far as I know, all our more distant relatives in the Baltics (the **Chaimovitch** family and the various **Rubinsteins** in Rīga and **Weidemanns** in Vilnius) perished in 1941.

---

us, it was simply hell, for the space was not sufficient for the people assembled. The Jews were ordered to stand with their faces toward the wall, and told not to move or look around for relatives or at the watchmen. The noise was earsplitting and the SD guards and the watchmen reacted with beatings and brutality."

COULD WE HAVE SAVED THEM?

For years, my mother tormented herself about my father's death, thinking up ways we might have saved him. Actually there was no realistic hope.

Hiding. At least 472 Latvian Jews tried to hide with compassionate Latvians, and some 300 were still alive when the Soviets re-occupied the country in 1944/45. But few Latvians were willing to assume the huge risk of hiding Jews and the huge burden of feeding them. In Western European countries (especially the Netherlands) people who were caught hiding Jews generally got off with brief prison terms, but in Eastern Europe they were sent to concentration camp (which few survived) or killed (especially if the Jews had weapons), often with their entire family. In contrast to several other countries, there was only a small guerrilla movement in Latvia, and even in those countries, Jewish volunteers often were not welcome, especially if they had no weapons.

One night in the winter of 1942/43 a Jewish woman who was hiding with a Latvian family rang our doorbell, having heard somehow that we were alive and living as Gentiles. (Unfortunately I have completely forgotten her name). She had to pay her hosts in jewelry from time to time, and although she carried everything on her, she pretended having to get it from some hiding place in town. Her life was very stressful; apart from the constant fear and the discomfort of living in a closet, she was often abused and spat upon by the hosts' little daughter. I think she visited us once more. After the war, my mother heard that this woman was found out and was last seen in a concentration camp in 1944, at which time she was showing signs of insanity.

New Identity. That was very difficult in a country where the police had been keeping records of every citizen. It was a long-shot option for a single young woman who didn't look Jewish, spoke Latvian like a native, and had courageous and resourceful Latvian friends who knew where and how to get false papers and how to get her settled in another town where nobody knew her. (Ezergailis, pp. 258–260, describes one such case, a single woman of 28.) It was a much riskier option for young men, as

they were circumcised (unlike gentile Latvians) and likely to be
drafted, where they would be seen naked by military doctors
and fellow soldiers. But it was out of the question for any of my
relatives, all of whom failed several of the above conditions.

Aryanization of Father. The Spektor family in Liepāja (whose
sons Eduard and Georg were our classmates) tried to save itself
by a story similar to ours. The mother Ella, who had a Russian
mother or grandmother, claimed that both her parents were
Russian, and managed to get SD-passes for herself and her sons.
But this left the father Josef vulnerable, and by November 1941,
they realized that he was doomed. In a desperate attempt to save
him, they now claimed that he was the illegitimate child of his
Jewish father and a gentile maid. But by November the SD had
become very leery of such stories, as the "gentile maid" usually
was said to be deceased. The younger son, Georg, then made
some change in his father's passport. However, the police
spotted the alteration, arrested first Georg for forgery and then
the rest of the family. None were ever seen again.[21]

The Spektors had overplayed their hand. Moreover, Russians
ranked too low in the Nazi racial hierarchy. Slavs were only a
notch above Jews, and according to the *Generalplan Ost* were to
be decimated and resettled, in order to make room for Germanic
settlers after the war. Half-Jews with Russian blood were not
worth preserving. Spilling blood of the German master race—
even if tainted by Jewish blood—was another matter, and thus
Erica's claim of a *German* origin may have saved our lives more
than once.

To Sweden. The Swedish island of Gotland was only 140 km
from Liepāja, and on very clear days, one could allegedly see the
chimney of a cement factory. In principle fishermen could carry
refugees across, but I doubt if more than a handful of Jews, if
any, escaped that way. Fuel was rationed, the coast was tightly
patrolled, and the boat's lengthy absence would have aroused
suspicion. A single anti-Semite among the fishermen could have

---

[21] A German Navy officer, Dr. Lancelle, had befriended the family and was
very upset to learn that they had been shot. At dinner in the officers' mess that
night he referred to it as "murder" and got into an argument with a Nazi
officer, Frenzel. Lancelle was court-martialed, demoted, and assigned to a
penal unit, followed by 3 months in a probationary unit at the front.

prevented all others from trying. Indeed, Linkimer in his diary mentions two people—teacher Leib Glikman (28) and a pharmacist's assistant, probably Hana Rebekka Zesman (28)— who had paid a fisherman for the trip but when they appeared at the appointed time and place, the SD was waiting for them. Lastly, there were rumors of refugees who had been killed, stripped, and tossed overboard on the high seas. As they necessarily carried all their valuables with them, this was an easy if messy way for a fisherman to collect his fare and a nice bonus without the inconvenience of a 280 km trip. My best friend in 5th grade was a fisherman's son, but it never occurred to us to contact his father.

6. PLAYING FOR TIME: 1942–44

3-MONTH REPRIEVES

SOON AFTER THE December massacre the SD confiscated our passes and told us to resolve our status with the office of the *Gebietskommissar* (District Commissioner, the German civilian administrator for Courland). The official handling such matters, Mr. Buttgereit, gave us a 3-month pass on the condition that my mother (1) divorce my father, (2) get two affidavits confirming her foundling story from people who had known it long before the war, and (3) locate a baptismal certificate proving her Christian origin.

My mother filed for divorce and soon obtained a ruling from the district court terminating the divorce proceedings "upon advice of the State Prosecutor that Adolfs Alperovičs had died on 9 December, 1941". This satisfied Mr. Buttgereit.

The first person we asked for an affidavit was our friend Herta Kārkliņš. She willingly agreed and made up the following story.

"...In the summer of 1930 I became acquainted with Erika Alperovičs. About a year later she told me that she is a foundling. A maid who worked for her Jewish adoptive parents had found Erika

Alperovičs, a couple months old, abandoned on the stairs. With the child there was a note, written in German, saying that the child was baptized Erika.

"The maid fervently begged the adoptive parents not to abandon the baby but to take it in and raise it as their own child. Thus Erika Alperovičs was raised in a Jewish family. But later, when Erika Alperovičs was older, the same maid disclosed her true origins to her. Learning the truth, she felt estranged from her adoptive parents and became very attached to the maid, who was Christian.

"Further Erika Alperovičs told me that she had not attended Jewish schools but had graduated from a Russian Gymnasium.

"In addition, I can attest that during the years we knew each other Erika Alperovičs and I together attended services in St. Anne's church, and that she also raised her sons Georgs and Eduards in a Christian spirit.

"The above-mentioned sons Georgs and Eduards did not attend Jewish schools but graduated from Čakste elementary school, after which they attended the Liepāja State Technicum. At home only the German language is used."

Herta had known us for a number of years and thus had a motive for saving us. But our second witness—Sofija Zīverts (63; Fig. 15)—was a virtual stranger who did it out of pure altruism. Her daughter, Lilija Jakšēvičs, had moved into our building in 1940, had resented the Soviet occupation no less than we did, and now deeply deplored the murder of Jews. It was her husband who had told me, outraged, about the shootings near the fishermen's wharf in early July. My mother felt free to approach her, and Mrs. Jakšēvičs willingly volunteered her mother as a false witness. I presume somebody helped her concoct the following story.

"About 40 years ago, I, Sofija Emilija Zīverts, née Brēdiķis, while visiting the beachside park, got to know the nursemaid Anna Freiers. After we had known each other for some time, she told me that the little girl Erika in her care is a foundling, who was adopted and raised as their own child by some Jewish family for whom Anna Freiers was working. Further Anna Freiers told me that she herself had found the baby, which was accompanied by a note saying that the girl had been baptized Erika. Anna Freiers and Erika visited me at home several times, whereupon Erika and my daughter Anna became close friends.

"After a break of several years, my daughter again began to see her friend Erika. This friendship continued until the [First] World War.

"In 1940, my daughter Lilija moved to Ulich Street 68, where Erika Alperovičs and her family lived in another apartment. Before long I met Erika Alperovičs in my daughter's apartment. After a short conversation she asked me whether I had another daughter named Anna, and after a few questions she recognized me as the mother of her childhood friend Anna."

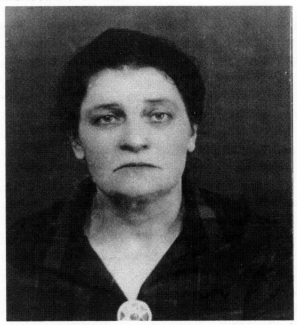

15. Sofija Zīverts (1928), who helped save us by a false affidavit

I think there are a few grains of truth in this story, but I do not remember exactly what they are. Mrs. Zīverts and little Anna may have casually known Erica and her nursemaid, but the friendship probably is an exaggeration and the foundling story is pure invention. Anyhow, thanks to these brave women, we had the required two affidavits.

The baptismal certificate was a tougher proposition. Records of all German churches in the Baltic countries had allegedly been removed to some archive in Poznań (Posen) in German-annexed western Poland (renamed Warthegau) in 1939–1941, when most ethnic Germans followed Hitler's call for repatriation—some more for fear of Stalin than love of Hitler. They were resettled mainly in the Warthegau. Mail between Liepāja and Poznań took 4–6 weeks each way in early 1942, so by the time our 3 months were up, we merely had a letter saying that the church records were not at the first address we had written to, but perhaps in another archive.

Mr. Buttgereit accepted the affidavits and gave us a 3-month extension on the condition that my mother locate her baptismal certificate by then. We soon heard from the archive, but the staff misunderstood our query and asked for exact information on birth date and -place, parents' names, etc. The 3 months were up before that misunderstanding was resolved. It also turned out that the church records were in Rīga after all. Mr. Buttgereit grudgingly extended our pass by 3 months, but warned us that this was the last time.

Georg had a business trip to Rīga in July 1942 and went to the archives. The Latvian State Historical Archives were closed to the public for an indefinite time, but he learned that the appropriate place actually was the State Vital Records Office. They were not yet open to the public but though heavily backlogged, would accept inquiries about a specific, fully identified person. For a vague search like ours we would have to wait until they allowed people to do searches on their own.

We doubted if Mr. Buttgereit would extend our exemption on so vague a prospect, and began to close our accounts with the world as the 3-month deadline approached. Erica's nerves were always at the breaking point before each of these deadlines. Even though Georg and I carefully scripted her little speech, she kept worrying how to answer every conceivable question. Georg and I felt that some of them were pretty far-fetched, but advised her as best we could. In our youthful optimism we thought that she was overreacting. Somehow we didn't fully appreciate that she bore most of the burden, having to do all the talking, and sensing that she might fail if logic rather than glibness was called for.

But when Erica and Georg went to Mr. Buttgereit's office on the appointed day, they learned that he had been transferred. His successor, Mr. Pusill, knew none of the background, and so Erica, aided by Georg, put a positive spin on the story, backtracking a few steps.

Curiously, this tactic worked at least once more, when Pusill was in turn transferred after two or three 3-month extensions. Meanwhile, the Vital Records Office in Rīga had reopened, and when Erica and I went there in the summer of 1943, we found that not only one but *two* girls indeed had been baptized Erika in the 3 months preceding my mother's birthday (alleged to be the day she was found by her "adoptive" parents). But the new man at the *Gebietskommissar's* office, Gutschmidt, was smart enough to realize that many years could be spent on inconclusive efforts to prove that my mother was in fact one of these girls, especially if she herself was conducting the search and able to suppress any inconvenient information. On 30 Sep 43 he therefore refused to renew our 3-month passes. Had he followed this decision to its logical and legal consequences, we would have been sent to the Šķēde dunes, or at best to the Rīga ghetto,[22] where only skilled craftsmen such as tailors had a chance of surviving. "Non-essential" Jews, including some from other parts of Europe, were selected out with increasing severity and shipped off to Auschwitz or killed locally in early November 1943.

We waited for the sword of Damocles to fall, wondering whether the police would arrest us at work or at home, and if the latter, by day or by night. Instead, nothing whatsoever happened. The local anti-Semites who had repeatedly denounced us to the police in 1941–42 had given up in discouragement, thinking that we had connections in the highest places—according to one rumor we heard, *none other than Hermann Göring's staff!*

Why Reichs-Marschall Göring (Hitler's #2), of all people? What may have triggered this rumor was that Erica worked as a part-time file clerk in a tiny, 4-person office, grandiloquently called:

Ostland Eisenhandelsgesellschaft m.b.H. der Reichswerke "Hermann Göring"

---

[22] A small, relatively benign ghetto existed in Liepāja from June 1942 to 8 October 1943, when the last ~800 inhabitants were deported to the Rīga ghetto. (Ezergailis, *Holocaust*, 298). At least some Latvians tried to help the Liepāja Jews; once, while passing the ghetto during a snowfall, I saw a light beam from the ghetto aimed at a window across the street, flashing signals in Morse code.

(Ostland Iron Trading Company Ltd. of the Reich Works „Hermann Göring".) It was merely a purchasing office channeling the production of the local wire factory to a giant industrial complex in Germany named after Göring. But an average Latvian seeing Erica going in and out of a building with this sign would choke on the big German words, and might conclude that she had a direct connection to Göring. I would have liked to thank the person who started the Göring rumor, as I could not have invented a better one myself.

A more real if passive protector was the Latvian police chief, Major Grauds. He must have doubted my mother's tale all along, because he had lived across the street from her parents. But although he did not want to risk issuing me an internal passport when I reached age 16 in 1942, he also did not lift a finger against us when we lost the last shred of German protection and entered a legal limbo.

As I learned only in 1997 from documents in the US Holocaust Memorial Museum, perhaps it was a good thing that Mr. Gutschmidt dropped us. Six months later, in April 1944, a staff officer of the Higher SS- and Police Chief Ostland wrote a draft directive, complaining that a substantial number of Jews in the Baltics had tried to evade their fate by claiming Aryan or part-Aryan birth from extramarital affairs of their parents, or from errors in church or vital records. Invariably, the persons alleged to have first-hand knowledge of the Aryan origin are dead, and thus the story rests entirely on dubious, self-serving testimony. The directive then accuses the *Generalkommissar* of being too gullible and lenient, and proposes all such cases to be turned over to the SD for investigation and decision. Being a police branch, the SD is much better qualified than a civilian *Generalkommissar* to examine such claims.

Several drafts of this directive exist, dated between April and July 1944. If this policy ever was formally adopted, unresolved cases such as ours would be obvious targets of the SD. Gutschmidt's decision to close our case may have been a way to avoid getting blood on his hands. Surely the SD would soon find out on its own that we had lost our protection. But by closing our case he had made us invisible.

LIFE GOES ON

Now back to January 1942. This was the darkest period of the war, on both the personal and the global level. The Nazis had killed >90% of the Jews in Latvia, making it clear that even the skilled workers still spared would have no place in Hitler's "New Europe". Instead of Kügler's permanent exemption we now had only a 3-month pass whose renewal depended on proof that we could never supply. The best we could hope for was that the Germans would lose the war before they lost their patience (with us).

But the war went disastrously for the Allies. The Japanese had dealt severe blows to the US Navy at Pearl Harbor and the Royal Navy at Singapore; had seized the Philippines, Burma, Indonesia, and Malaysia; and continued to hop, unstoppably, from island to island. The Germans had reached the outskirts of Moscow in October, and although they were stopped in December by the bitter cold and a Soviet counteroffensive, they had captured nearly 4 million Soviet prisoners, and seemed set to finish off the Soviet Union the following summer.[23]

We hoped against all odds that heavenly justice and the military might of the Allies would eventually prevail, and focused most of our thoughts on the here and now. Food rations were skimpy, but more generous than in Ukrainian cities such as Kharkov and Kiev, where thousands died of starvation each month during the 1941/42 winter. In the Nazi racial hierarchy, Latvians ranked several notches above the bottom (Latvians > Lithuanians > Ukrainians > Poles & Russians >> Jews), and thus were not treated quite as badly. If memory serves, we got 300 g meat and 200 g butter per month, as well as almost adequate amounts of potatoes, cabbage, and bread. The bread was dark, coarse, and very moist and sticky (allegedly extended with potatoes); all the choicer fruits, berries, vegetables, and fish had vanished; and of the cheapest local fish—cod—only the heads

---

[23] In July 1941, the Germans had burned tens or hundreds of thousands of Red Army felt boots in Liepāja. They expected the war to end soon, and knowing that the Red Army had, well, a chronic problem with lice, they did not consider recycling worth the trouble. The German soldiers would have appreciated these boots in December.

were still available. (One more step in this disappearing act and the cod would have vanished like the Cheshire cat, with only the grin remaining.) Fortunately Latvian farmers were very productive and managed to maintain a thriving black market throughout the war. By bartering my father's clothes and other expendables we avoided starvation.

To continue my education as best I could, I enrolled in a home study course at the *Rustin Institut für Fernunterricht* (Rustin Institute for Home Study) in Potsdam. Owing to wartime shortages, I received only a fraction of the 300-odd booklets comprising the civil engineering technician's course (again, without exact equivalent in the US, but closer to a high school than a college program). However, the Institute promptly supplied me with an impressive ID card, bearing a large Prussian eagle. Though matching neither the fluffy imperial eagle of the Second Reich nor the swastika-clutching, stylized bird of the Third Reich, it had an intimidating, official look about it, which enabled this innocuous correspondence school ID to serve as my passport in critical moments.

My Latvian friends treated me as their equal, and so did their friends. They never dropped the slightest hint that I was a second-class citizen; on the contrary, they made it clear that they did not accept Nazi racial doctrines. However, I felt it necessary to avoid girls. If they somehow found out that I was circumcised, they would be able to destroy me. Fortunately, I was quite awkward and shy with girls, having been in sex-segregated classes since age 10.

We again had roomers in our apartment, as we needed the money. The first was a former Latvian diplomat, Nikolajs Āboltiņš, who then moved to Rīga and graciously hosted us during our 1943 visit to the Rīga archives. (At his home we met several upper class Latvians and a German soldier, all of whom detested the Nazis). Then came two German railroad men, Fischer and Wildenhain. The latter moved out after a year, and Fischer's wife [from Chomutov (Komotau) in the Sudetenland] came for a couple of months. We treated her well, not knowing that she would do us a big favor in 1944 (Fig. 16).

16. *Mrs. Fischer, I, and Erica (Summer 1943)*

After the Fischers left, we got a Mr. Hansen from Hamburg. One of Hansen's eccentricities was his bed, comprising 7 layers of sheets, blankets, and comforters. Before going to bed he checked the thermometer to decide into which layer to crawl.

One of Hansen's friends from Germany planned to visit him shortly before Christmas 1943 and asked him to get a goose that he could take back to his family. Hansen made the arrangements through his black-market contacts, but the farmer delivered the eviscerated goose a bit too soon, in early December. Though we had no refrigerator, our cellar usually was cold enough in the winter. But as luck would have it, the weather turned unseasonably warm, and the goose got smelly. Erica conferred with Hansen, and between them they decided to rub the goose with garlic to mask the odor. A few days later the friend arrived, and I overheard Hansen explain the garlic massage with the words, "You know, this used to be a Jewish household". The friend assured him of his full understanding and left happily with the goose, perhaps proud of his ecumenical spirit.

Hansen once gave me a good scare. We were desperate for news from the Allies, and had therefore bartered some of our belongings for a radio soon after the German policeman Lemke had confiscated our set in 12/41. It was an old, mediocre AM set with poor selectivity and no shortwave. The Germans jammed all 4± BBC stations, but occasionally one or the other became intelligible over the *wawawawa…* din. AM radio has a very short

range until after dark, so we had to do our listening in the
evenings when Hansen—a Nazi party member—was home. To
muffle the sound, I always covered the radio with a comforter
and crouched under it, but as I emerged from this "tent" one
evening, I heard Hansen in the kitchen shouting to my mother,
"but I have told him...." I thought he had heard the telltale
wawawawa... even through the comforter and two closed doors,
and was now going to turn us in. But he was merely letting off
steam about some third party. That was fortunate, as listening to
foreign radio stations was punishable by death.

Hansen eventually got his own radio. He brought two
models home and asked me which one to keep. I promptly put
my foot in my mouth by opting for the one with shortwave, but
he looked at me uncomprehendingly and asked, "what for?" I do
not recall how I extricated myself, but luckily he indeed kept
that one. After the Normandy landings in June 1944, I would
sneak into his room after work to listen to the BBC, always being
careful to tune the set back to his favorite German station. Once
or twice I heard his key in the door when I was still listening,
and though I re-tuned the set and scrammed before he walked
in, I was scared to death he might notice that the (vacuum-tube!)
set was warm if he happened to turn it on right away. Still, the
risk seemed worth it. A few days after the landings, when the
Germans still bragged about a counterattack any moment that
would sweep the Allies back into the sea, we heard on the BBC
that King George VI had visited the beachhead. That convinced
us that the beachhead was safe; like chess players, countries do
not knowingly endanger their king.

WORK

After the December 1941 massacre, I continued to look for a
job, helped by a kind and compassionate Latvian in the
Employment Office. The first job he found for me—in a Latvian
office—lasted only a few days, until they discovered that I was
classified as a half-Jew. I had no better luck in the second job
(early January 1942) as an office messenger at the
Marinehafenbauabteilung (Naval Port Construction Department).
The boss was German but the staff was Latvian. One of my

errands took me to *Schutzpolizei* (Order Police) headquarters, where a German officer, impressed by my fluent German, offered to enlist me on the spot in the Latvian *Schutzmannschaften* (the same auxiliary police that only a month ago had rounded us up for execution; some of them had even served on execution squads). He was already talking of *einkleiden* (=fitting me for a uniform) when I modestly disqualified myself as an underage (15 ½) half-Jew. He was visibly disappointed. Perhaps he told my (German) boss, who soon discharged me, having learned of my non-Aryan background. Actually I was not sorry to leave, as the atmosphere had become somewhat uncongenial. Once when I was in the room, the accountant pointedly told his colleagues: "Do you know that we are all drinking the blood of Jews now? Their blood has seeped into the ground and now is in our drinking water."

Fortunately, the local branch of the construction firm *A. Dehlert* from Danzig was willing to hire me in 2/42 as a junior clerk and draftsman, having previously hired Georg for a similar position. The boss (Paul Schlicht), though a simple-minded, loyal Nazi, completely rejected Hitler's anti-Semitism, and resolutely protected us later when an army major wanted us barred from a construction project.

My duties gradually expanded, and eventually included the payroll for 80 workers. This had been a full-time job for a young woman, who laboriously calculated each case on a hand-cranked calculator and then transferred the information separately onto 3 forms rather than making carbons. In an early manifestation of my optimizing urge, I figured out the proper way to do data entry on the system (designed by the US efficiency expert Frederick Winslow Taylor), and avoided repetitive calculations by making up a table of gross wages for any hourly rate and number of hours. Now the payroll took only half a day. However, my own pay was lousy (by law, a teenager got only 60% of an adult's wage).

Even with these additional duties, I had plenty of spare time. Several times my boss sent me to Rīga on "business" trips for quite trivial reasons (once I was to get two earthenware bowls for use as wash basins; they were available in Rīga but not

Liepāja). Military trains had priority, so the trip of normally 5 hrs now took at least 18 hrs, and as I usually returned on the same day, it generally meant two nights on the crowded train. When I was lucky, I was able to stretch out on the overhead baggage rack; otherwise I had to sit up.

Soon I learned to get some personal benefit from these trips. The main Liepāja-Rīga line passed through a short stretch of Lithuania, where the Lithuanian farmers were eager to barter farm products for nails—unavailable in Lithuania but plentiful in Liepāja, thanks to the local wire factory. Early in the morning on the way back to Liepāja, the train stopped in open country where the farmers were waiting, and moved on after the passengers had bartered hardware for food.

I was in Rīga on 26 July 1943 when the local newspaper carried a brief (2 column-inch) story with a tiny headline, "New Government in Italy". Toned down as it was, the message came through: Mussolini had been deposed and arrested, and Marshal Badoglio had formed a new government without fascists! This was the latest in a string of setbacks for the Nazis: Stalingrad in January, surrender in North Africa in May, Allied landings in Sicily in early July. Now the famous Axis alliance had cracked. Clutching my bowls and nails I got on the train and daydreamed happily until nail-trading time, not expecting that the war would last nearly another 2 years.

Often I was sent on errands to the Naval Base north of town, where our company had several construction projects. Feeling underpaid, I extended these trips by a few hours, especially when the weather was nice. I had a special pass to enter the base area, and somehow Zigurds and another of my school friends got such passes as well. Together we strolled through the open pine forest, looking for abandoned Soviet weapons. We did not dare collect any rifles, but marveled at their simple construction, which made them much easier to disassemble and clean than the WWI Ross-Enfield rifles that we had used in military class in elementary school. But being insouciant teenagers we helped ourselves to some equally well-designed hand grenades and tracer bullets.

While Zigurds ' parents were at work in the theater we examined the ordnance we had found on the Naval Base. The tracer bullets (pulled out of the cartridge) hissed and popped nicely when thrown into the stove, imparting beautiful colors to the flames. Lacking detonators, the hand grenades were less dramatic, but we took one apart, removed the wax-like, hollow cylinder of explosive, and ignited several small pieces. As expected, they burned vigorously but did not explode.

Dumb teenagers that we were, we wondered what additional weaponry might exist in the Artillery Laboratory compound, a fenced-in, guarded area on the Naval Base. One day we crawled through the barbed wire and began to explore the wooded area. Not having found anything interesting, we crossed the road, hoping to have better luck on the other side. As we glanced to the right, we saw two rifle-bearing German sentries at a distance, coming toward us. We retreated into the woods, but they intercepted us before we had reached the fence. Somehow we talked our way out of this predicament, but one sentry said we were lucky not to have trespassed during the previous shift, as that patrol fired right away. They had reason to be wary; German soldiers were occasionally shot at in Liepāja.

Georg had become assistant foreman and usually was at the construction sites in the Naval Base. At one of the rather frequent drinking parties the other assistant foreman, O.(svalds?) Kārkliņš (no relation to Herta), became violent and beat up Georg. We decided to prepare for a re-match. Georg had learned a fair amount of metalworking at school and had forged a beautiful 6" hunting knife from a broken automobile spring. Now he cast elegant aluminum knuckles for himself and made a cruder version for me, consisting of two C-shaped metal rods held together with wire.

The re-match came when Kārkliņš appeared in the office one day, shouting: "What's the matter, Jews, won't we get paid today?" (Or some similar complaint, I don't remember). Georg and I attacked him with our knuckles, he fought back with a steel ruler he had grabbed from a desk, and by the time people separated us a few seconds later, Kārkliņš had a number of cuts and bruises whereas I had a few scratches. The police came, confiscated our weapons (including the knife, which Georg wisely had not used), and made out a report.

A court case and trouble with the police was the last thing we needed. We hired a lawyer who advised me to get a doctor's report on my scratches. That was a smart move, as the report looked much gorier than I did, enabling our lawyer to file a countersuit. A few weeks later in court, the attorneys for the two parties proposed a settlement: we were to pay damages of RM 300 (about 4 months' wages), of which Kārkliņš was to donate RM 100 to charity. Naturally we accepted, although Georg begrudged the loss of his knife.

I do not remember details, but we also had an unpleasant encounter with the foreman, Klamers. But before long he did himself in. After another drinking party on the Naval Base, he grabbed a rifle from one of the workers guarding Soviet POWs and pointed it at a German soldier. He was arrested and put in a prison cell, where he hanged himself by his belt during the night. In an ironic twist, Georg was appointed his successor.

That required Georg to be outdoors much of the time. Once he told me that he had sabotaged a railroad car by putting gravel into the oil chambers of the wheels, which could have caused a derailment when the bearings overheated. I do not know how often he did that.

Next to Jews, Soviet POWs were the most persecuted group in Nazi Europe. By February 1942, only 1.1 million of the 3.9 million POWs captured up to that time were still alive, the others having died of cold, disease, starvation, or deliberate killing. Only about half a million survived the war. They were kept out of public view, and only once did I catch a glimpse of their miserable condition. When two German sailors on the Naval Base dumped a barrel of (apparently spoiled) sauerkraut in front of a group of emaciated POWs, the POWs, abandoning all human dignity, fell onto it like a pack of hungry animals. I was shocked to see one of them crawling away on all fours like a dog, a fistful of sauerkraut hanging out of his mouth. A year later 10 POWs worked in the back yard of our office, guarded by our boss' chauffeur. He asked me to take his rifle and watch the prisoners for half an hour while he went out on an errand. I have regretted ever since that I did not give them my lunch. Though not as starved as the earlier group, they surely were not overfed and needed bread more than I did. Yes, there were severe penalties for helping POWs (a half-Jew, Ateres Aronson, was arrested and shot in January 1945 for giving bread to POWs), but I had taken greater risks for lesser reasons.

I learned little science during that time, except for some dabblings in rock analysis that were cut short by lack of the necessary reagents. But I found out how to make potassium cyanide from harmless chemicals, and Erica and I always carried a couple of grams with us, in case we got into a difficult situation.

PRIVATE FRITZ MÜLLER

My intellectual development also stagnated for a year, when I read mainly trash, from dime novels to the viciously anti-Semitic weekly *Der Stürmer*. Fortunately, I met an outstanding individual in 1942, the architect Fritz Müller (1906–1980) from Stuttgart, then a private in a construction battalion of the German army that was stationed in Liepāja 1942/43 and contracted some projects to the construction firm where I worked. Müller was an anti-Nazi idealist who regularly gave 6/7 of his weekly bread ration to Jews and never used the sidewalk after Jews had been forbidden to use it. His comrades knew how strongly he empathized with Jews and occasionally teased him: "Müller looks so sad today, he must have seen a Jew." He often visited us at home, became a father figure to me, and gently steered me away from trash toward good music and literature. Among the books I read on his recommendation were the Bildungsroman *Wilhelm Meister's Lehr- und Wanderjahre* [Wilhelm Meister's Apprenticeship and Travels] by Goethe and the historic novel *Jürg Jenatsch* by C.F. Meyer. People like Müller and Schlicht have taught me *never* to condemn a whole group for the crimes of some of its members.

Müller once startled me by declaring that in his opinion, it would be no calamity if the German nation ceased to exist after the end of the war. It turned out he meant not physical destruction of individuals but disappearance of the German nation-state. We did not pursue the question further, especially whether Germany should come under foreign rule or merely revert to an assortment of mini-states, as before 1871. But his remark made me realize that individuals are more important than nations, as expressed in overly extreme form by an Englishman who said: "If I had the choice of betraying my friend or betraying my country, I hope I will have the courage to betray my country." Though both choices are thoroughly repugnant to me, they are not as bad as the blindly loyal "Right or wrong, my country".

17. Fritz Müller, drafting in Liepāja (1942). 18. Probably in Russia (1943/44)

Müller was a follower of *anthroposophy*, a spiritual philosophy based on the teachings of Rudolf Steiner (1861–1925). It is rooted in Christianity, somewhat akin to Rosicrucianism, but less mystical, more cerebral. Famous followers include Saul Bellow, Bruno Walter, and Albert Schweitzer.

> I located Müller in Stuttgart after the war and was able to share some of our food parcels with him. He had been taken prisoner by the Red Army near the end of the war, but was released relatively soon. We saw each other a few times before I left for the US. Only in 2006 did I try to track him down and succeeded with the help of the *Goetheanum* in Dornach, Switzerland, the world center of anthroposophy. Müller had died in 1980, but I obtained an obituary from the director of the archive, Uwe Werner, and a few pictures (Fig. 17, 18) from Müller's only daughter, Dr. Christa Müller in Stuttgart.

From the obituary I learned that Müller throughout his life had remained the same compassionate, generous, and idealistic man I had known in 1942. Here are some quotes. *"Müller became a very successful architect after the war, building, among others, 400 schools. He designed and donated two buildings for the Goetheanum, modestly remaining in the background afterwards. He was a man who could not live without helping others. He had a special gift that enabled him to sense other people's worries and their causes, as well as crises in human relations. In later years he developed intensive contacts with Israel. Shortly before his death he was invited to Argentina to discuss future projects."*

I was amazed to learn from Christa Müller that he did all this prodigious work from a small office, with a staff of only two.

Schopenhauer's *Aphorisms*, which my mother gave me, got me interested in philosophy. Trying to be eccentric, I read a book on my way to work every morning, never lifting my eyes to check where the curb was. Sometimes I got up early, to have time for a quick dip in the Baltic. Once there were bits of ice floating in the water, but that did not deter me.

GEORG IS DRAFTED

As their military situation deteriorated during 1942–43, the Germans became more and more willing to accept help from previously disdained ethnic groups. In February 1943, soon after Stalingrad, Hitler ordered formation of a "Latvian Volunteer Legion". The poorly equipped and dressed Latvian police battalions of 1942 (partly volunteer), which had served mainly in brutal anti-partisan warfare, now were upgraded. Some of them became the nucleus of the two combat divisions of the Legion, augmented mainly by draftees. Cleverly, the Nazis organized the Legion under the Waffen-SS rather than the Army.[24]

The German Waffen-SS divisions organized in the 1930s and early 1940s were elite units, composed of handpicked Nazis of purest Aryan blood (going back 6 generations rather than the usual 3). Heavily indoctrinated and led by fanatical officers, they committed many war crimes against civilians and POWs. But starting in 1941,

---

[24] Heinrich Himmler, supreme leader of the SS, missed no opportunity to increase his power by getting more people under his command. Another reason may have been that—as a Russian soldier told me after the war—Russians usually shot on the spot any captive with SS insignia; knowing this policy, SS units tended to fight to the last man.

Germany began to establish military units of foreigners, first of Germanic peoples (Dutch, Norwegians, Danes, Flemings, Walloons) then of non-Germanic peoples, including some former enemies (Latvians, Estonians, Croats, Albanians, French, Turks, even British). These foreign units were assigned to the Waffen-SS, but did not have to meet the racial and ideological criteria of the German units. Originally having the words "Legion" and *"Freiwillige"* (volunteer) in their names, these foreign units were later renamed to indicate their lower status by a subtle variation in word order. Whereas German units had SS at the start of the name (*SS Panzerdivision Hohenstaufen*), the foreign ones had it at the end (*15. Waffen-Grenadier-Division der SS*). "...der SS" = "of the SS" implies that they were subordinate to the SS, not part of it. Their uniforms usually had some decorative emblem on the collar instead of the SS runes, and in their rank designations "SS" was replaced by the meaningless "Waffen" (arms). All these foreign units had German SS officers in the top command positions. The question of their involvement in atrocities will be discussed in Part II. Still, to this day they continue to be stigmatized by the SS affiliation.

Georg's year (1924) was called up in March 1943, but he was temporarily deferred. On November 8, 1943, he was drafted into the 20th Latvian Police Battalion, of all places! (Fig. 19). As a putative half-Jew, he was assigned to a "labor company" of racial dregs, such as gypsies, Ukrainians, Lithuanians, and Latvian-born ethnic Poles. Their Latvian lieutenant, while drunk, gave a speech candidly discussing future plans for the unit. "Labor company" was merely a code name; they would be sent into the fiercest combat and only those who proved themselves would have a place in Hitler's "New Europe". But those who didn't—beware! Theft by gypsies was rampant, so Georg's wallet and a few other belongings soon disappeared.

Five weeks later the German liaison officer of the battalion decided, however, that recruiting standards had been lowered too far, and discharged Georg on December 14,[25] overruling the Latvian company and battalion commanders who had endorsed his petition to stay in the unit.

---

[25] Nazi policy toward half-Jews was inconsistent and kept changing with time and from place to place. According to a high-level directive, half-Jews were ineligible for military service, as the Nazis wanted free hand to deal with them after the war without feeling obligated for their help in securing "final victory". Indeed, some documents show that all half-Jews were to be killed after the war. But Hitler had famously declared: "I am the one who decides who is a Jew" and had knowingly kept some part-Jewish officers, such as Air Marshal Milch.

Georg's draft board promptly wanted to induct him again and assign him to the Latvian Legion, in the hope that they might be less choosy. But he came down with typhoid fever, was hospitalized, and contracted diphtheria. Then he became delirious. On 14 January 1944, I had met Mr. Hansen on my way home from work, and when we entered the kitchen together, I asked my mother why she was making such a terrible face. "Georg died this afternoon", she said. Without a word I rushed into my bedroom, but Mr. Hansen followed me, trying to comfort me as best he could.

19. *Georg in the old (blue) German police uniform that was issued to his battalion (early Dec. 1943).*   **20.** *My mood in the months after Georg's death is evident in this picture (February or March 1944).*

Georg's death hurt me more than any previous loss, because we had become very close friends after years of squabbling. I still have the affectionate letters he wrote during his 5 weeks in the military. Erica, who had visited him daily in the hospital, claimed that poor care by anti-Semitic personnel was at least a contributing factor, but I doubt this.[26] The day before his death

---

[26] A German Jew who was in Liepāja for several months in 1942/43 and visited an injured friend in the City Hospital, reports that the friend was getting very good care, apparently people had pity for him. The nurse brought him everything he asked for, the doctor gave him competent treatment, and the

he, already delirious, called out to her: "Mommy, Mommy, I had to climb over a Mountain of Death!"

Erica was even more affected by Georg's death than I was and had to quit her job. Both of us were pained by the sight of his clothes and other belongings, and by the constant thought that we had lost him forever. Realizing that I could not run away from my grief I decided to face it head-on in the weeks after his death, and retraced our various hikes in the countryside. That had the cathartic effect I had hoped for.

The minister at the German Evangelical church, Rev. E. Bahn, nobly agreed to conduct funeral services for Georg, although we had never attended his church. Fewer than a dozen people came to the graveside ceremony, where Bahn alluded with candor and sympathy to our family's sufferings. I ordered a headstone (from a marble switchboard plate I had found in an electrical supply store) but it was not done when we left Liepāja later that year and apparently was never installed. When we visited Central Cemetery in Liepāja in 1998, we found that untended graves are reassigned after 40 years, so Georg's gravesite was assigned to a Rāts family. I know nothing about this particular family, but an Olga and Jānis Rāts hid 2 Jews from late 1944 to early 1945. I hope it is the same family.

As the law provided, with the death certificate we received coupons for 3 bottles of vodka for the traditional funeral repast. Of course, we bartered them for food instead. In a bit of black humor soon after the funeral a policeman appeared at our door, ready to arrest Georg for failing to appear before the draft board. After hearing that Georg had died he cheerfully assured us that in that case, „everything is in order." We mentioned that Georg had been discharged from the police battalion, but he assured us that the Latvian Legion was less choosy.

Latvian patients in the ward shared any food brought by their families. [Josef Katz, *Erinnerungen eines Überlebenden*, Kiel: Neuer Malik Verlag (1988), 110.] One cannot easily generalize anecdotal information, but as even a few anti-Semites in an institution can intimidate the rest of the staff, the anti-Semites must have been limited in number and influence.

THE WAR 1942–44

Germany still looked nearly invincible in 1942. After losing some territory in the Soviet winter offensive 41/42, the Germans struck again in May 1942, penetrating deep into Southern Russia and the Caucasus. In the Atlantic, their U-Boats sank Allied ships faster than they could be built. In the West, Germany held the entire European continent, and when a British-Canadian force landed at Dieppe in Northern France in August 1942, it was wiped out in 9 hours. Britain had scored a small success in North Africa in 1941 by capturing the Libyan cities Tobruk and Benghazi from the Italians, but when Germany sent Field Marshal Rommel and his Africa Corps to Libya, he recaptured both cities and drove deep into Egypt. Wasn't there *anybody* who could stand up to the Germans??

Every few days, the German radio whipped up public enthusiasm by dramatic radio announcements of their latest victories. First they broke into the regular program to announce that a special bulletin of the High Command was forthcoming, and played military marches to set the mood for the dramatic moment 20 or 30 minutes later. Then came the bulletin, preceded and followed by a fanfare: half a million tons of shipping sunk, another Soviet city captured, a few more Soviet divisions wiped out, a record number of Allied planes shot down, etc. Erica, in particular, was desperate for good news, but there was little even on the BBC.

The tide turned late in the year. The British 8th Army under Montgomery counterattacked in Libya, US and British troops under Eisenhower landed in Algeria and Morocco, and the Soviets started their winter offensive, culminating in the capitulation of the German 6th Army at Stalingrad on 31 Jan 1943. That was a big blow to German prestige and self-esteem, to which Goebbels responded by declaring "Total War" two weeks later. We could not wholeheartedly cheer the Soviets, but were delighted that the Germans were not invincible after all. Several German generals captured at Stalingrad formed a "Free Germany Committee" (presumably under coercion), which urged the German people to end the war. The Soviets set up powerful transmitters that broke into German programs during brief pauses, broadcasting these appeals as well as slogans and news bites. We did not trust this propaganda, but were pleased to see that German airwaves, like German air space, were no longer inviolable.

The slogans had a distinct communist flavor and were more notable for their rhymes than for their content: *Schlagt die Nazibande tot, dann habt Ihr Frieden und Brot* [Kill the Nazi gang, then you'll have peace and bread], or *Der Krieg ist für die Reichen, das Volk liefert die Leichen* [War is for the rich, people supply the corpses].

Germany continued to slip in 1943, at a gradually accelerating pace. Their summer offensive in the USSR fizzled, and they continued to lose ground. German propaganda always put the best face on these retreats by bragging that they had "shortened front lines". Soon a political joke circulated that the Army was looking for several types of artisans; one of them was "tailors for shortening front lines". US and British air raids on Germany intensified, and Allied defenses against U-Boats were improving. But there was only modest progress in the one area that mattered to us most: Allied landings on the European continent. After liberating Sicily, the Allies landed on the Italian mainland, but although Italy changed sides and joined the Allies in September 1943, the Germans regained control and stopped the Allies north of Naples. (As Eisenhower wrote later, "…there were scores of vital points [in the terrain] where a battalion could stop an army's advance.") At the rate the Allies were progressing, it would have taken decades to liberate Europe from the south.

It was mid-morning on 6 June 1944 (D-Day) when Erica appeared in my office, trying hard to suppress a grin. She had come to the office every 3 months in 1942/43, to let me know that our pass had been extended, but this time she wanted to tell me that the Allies had landed in Normandy! She had only heard this on the German radio, but despite the heavy slant, we knew that this was not going to be another Dieppe. Hansen was out of town, and I could hardly wait to go home to get the BBC on shortwave.

Hitler (or Goebbels?) had bragged only a few months ago "next time the Allies land on the continent, they'll be lucky if they can hold out for 9 hours [as at Dieppe in 1942]". But not only had the Allies thrown sufficient forces into the battle, they also fooled the Germans by elaborate deception into believing that the Normandy landings were a feint, with the real invasion to come at Calais where the English Channel is at its narrowest. Accordingly, the Germans had massed their 15th Army at Calais, waiting in vain. The light did not dawn on them for nearly 2 months: Goebbels wrote an editorial saying that the Allies had landed most of their seasoned troops in Normandy and would have to rely on green troops for their second and third landings.

However, six weeks later the Allies were still bottled up in Normandy, and we feared another stalemate like that in Italy. But in the evening of 20 July we were electrified by the German radio report of the failed plot against Hitler, followed by a short speech by Hitler himself ("a very tiny clique..."). We deeply regretted the failure of the plot and the savage and widespread retribution that would now follow. Some 4,000 people involved in the plot were tried and executed. Even the celebrated hero of North Africa, Field Marshal Rommel, was involved in the plot. As the German public would have been very upset to learn that this hero had turned against Hitler, he was persuaded to kill himself. His death was attributed to strafing by enemy aircraft and he received a state funeral.

This plot was a most encouraging sign of inner rot at a time when the Western Allies had only two toeholds on the continent and the Germans were firing V1 and V2 rockets at Britain, with threats of *much worse* to follow.

Five days later (25 July 44) Allied tanks broke through German lines at Avranches and swept through France. Our spirits rose. But just then, things were heating up close to home. The Soviets had started their summer offensive on 23 June, and after smashing the German Army Group Center in Byelorussia, they crossed the Latvian border on 18 July. Now the war had moved into our back yard.

7. LEAVING LATVIA: 1944

T̲HE RED ARMY pushed swiftly into Latvia after the border crossing. They reached the Gulf of Rīga, cutting off Army Group North, and on 28 July their advance units were close to Jelgava, 170 km east of Liepāja. At the rate they were advancing, we feared they might reach Liepāja in a few days. (Actually the Germans were able to hold Liepāja until the very end of the war.) My year (1926) had to report for induction the very next day, 29 July, but with the Red Army surging forward, only about 8 draftees out of a pool of some 400 showed up. Not daring to take any chances, I went, passed my physical (as any cripple would at that stage of the war) but was saved from immediate induction by my non-Aryan background. The captain wanted to check with Latvian Legion headquarters in Rīga before putting me in uniform, and gave me a deferment (Fig. 21). Another boy who had shown up and was deferred for the same reason was Michael Aronson, son of a Jewish father and a Greek mother. He, too, did not dare to play hookey.[27]

---

[27] I spoke to him in 2000 when I visited Liepāja, and found that he had never been drafted although all deferments had been canceled in November 1944.

Apliecība

Šīs apliecības uzrādītājs *Alperovičs Eduards*

dzimis __21.6.26__ , ar dzīves vietu __Liepājā__

Ūliḥa ielā 68-i ir ieradies izpildīt karaklausību,

un ar __Liepājas SS-kara__ apriņķa karaklausības komisijas

__1944.__ g. __29. jūlijā__ lēmumu atzīts par derīgu darbā uz

__service minimie pamata__ pamata un kā tāds nav

iesaukšanas saraksta kārtējais Nr. *1*

194_4_ g. _29. jūlijā_ Nr. *2 / ž*

Kreis__

pirkst__   SS-kara apr. komandieris v.

Domlau__   Rīgā, Doma lauk. 1. 1199—17667.

21. *My draft deferment from the SS-Replacement Command Latvia. It confirms that I showed up "to fulfill [my] military service obligation" but was "not inducted by special order". The file number is 2/ž, where the ž apparently is an abbreviation of „žīds" = Jew.*

GETTING PAPERS

With the Soviets again on Latvian soil, the Germans offered to let trustworthy refugees seek "temporary" asylum in Germany, until the expected "final victory". I immediately recognized this as our only opportunity to be liberated by the Western Allies, because there was not a ghost of a chance that Eisenhower or Montgomery would get to Liepāja before Zhukov did. And one year under Stalin had been enough! Moreover, the Germans viewed this as a loyalty test: those who stayed were suspected of being communist sympathizers. We could not afford coming under such suspicion.

There was a minor difficulty: prospective refugees had to get clearance from the Latvian police, to make sure that only trustworthy people with a clean record entered Germany. Even if the police had been willing to let bygones be bygones and ignore their murders of my family, there was the utter illegitimacy of our situation. We no longer had a pass exempting us from the laws against Jews, and I had no passport, though required to have one since I had turned 16 in 1942. Nonetheless, I applied.

Every hour a policeman emerged from the headquarters building and called out the names of people whose applications had been processed. Not wanting our names to be called more than once, I waited there all day. I shall never know what security risks the police were trying to exclude and what files they checked, because when our names were called, the forms bore a rubber stamp: "No objections to departure". My clearance was overridden by a second stamp saying that as a male between 16 and 60 I was not allowed to leave. But at least we were now able to apply for an entry permit for my mother. Erica vehemently protested that she did not want to leave without me, but I took her passport and went to the *Gebietskomissar's* office.

Some time before, I had partly "aryanized" Erica's passport by erasing her Hebrew middle name (Rachel) with sodium hypochlorite (Fig. 22). The reagent nicely bleached the ink but also changed the pale blue background pattern to buff. I spread the hypochlorite over the entire lower right corner to make it look like a coffee spill, and similarly treated the corners of the next few pages. Then I neutralized the hypochlorite with sodium thiosulfate and burnished the paper with talcum powder. Though I knew that Georg Spektor and his family had been shot for similar doctoring, I gave it no further thought, being a typically insouciant teenager. That still left my mother's double maiden name (Šeftelovics-Lēventals), of which the first part looked very Jewish or Slavic, and the second part probably Jewish to a Latvian but less so to a German who might not recognize it as the Latvian spelling of the (very Jewish) "Löwenthal".[28]

---

[28] When Jews in Germany and Austria were required to get surnames from the police, anti-Semitic officials would assign funny-sounding names such as Knoblauch (garlic), Süsskind (sweet child), or Blechmann (sheet metal man). But even the less bigoted officers assigned distinctive names that, though German, were all but unknown among gentiles. The roots generally were precious metals or stones (Gold-, Silber-, Rubin-, Diamant-), wild animals (Löwen-, Wolf-, Bären-), or flowers (Blumen-, Lilien-, Rosen-), usually combined with suffixes such as –mann, -tal, -stein, -berg. Sometimes a bribe bought a better choice.

Standing in line and surveying the 3 girls that were issuing entry permits, I chose the one that seemed the slowest and densest, and crossed over to her line. Sure enough, she got confused by my mother's double name and let me dictate what to put on the entry permit. At my suggestion she omitted the more obviously-Jewish "Šeftelovics" and listed the ethnicity as

22. *Erica's passport, after deletion of her Jewish name "Rahile"(Rachel) on the bottom line with sodium hypochlorite.*

"*Volksdeutsche*" (ethnic German), thus producing an ID-card that was significantly aryanized relative to the passport. Alas, the story began to unravel when we took the document to her German boss for signature. Spotting "*Volksdeutsche*", he asked whether Erica had registered with Miss XYZ (who apparently kept a register of authenticated ethnic Germans). I said no, whereupon he yelled at the poor girl that nobody was to be classified as ethnic German who was not so registered. He made her cross out "*Volksdeutsche*" and write "*Lettland*" alongside, but not liking her penmanship, he barked, "no swine can read this". His fury spent, he failed to notice the omission of "Šeftelovics" and signed the document.

FORTRESS COURLAND

With the Soviets at the gates of Rīga, the Germans decided to make the western part of Latvia (Courland or Kurzeme) into a redoubt. Like other non-essential personnel I was laid off (31 Aug 44), and from 17 September on Erica and I had to dig trenches for "Fortress Courland". Every morning between 6 and 7 several narrow-gauge freight trains took workers to the defense perimeter where we dug into the hard, clayey soil all day, getting home around 8 PM. We rode in open boxcars, covering our faces against the showers of sparks from the coal-dust-fired engine. After 4 days, I had developed tendonitis in my ankle, whereupon a German medic excused me from further digging, certifying that I was suitable only for "light work". I suspect he was influenced by my fluent German and my knowledge of medical terms such as *"Sehnenscheidenentzündung"* (tendonitis), which I had looked up in an encyclopædia. Erica was tougher and continued to dig trenches for another week or two.

Life in Liepāja became bleaker. Soviet air raids became heavier and more frequent. During the first 3 years, there had been only a few minor (daytime) raids involving at most 2–3 Soviet planes that dropped a few small bombs haphazardly. Air raid sirens usually gave 5–10 minutes' warning, unless the planes came in from the sea. But now the raids became heavier, if still poorly targeted, and came at all hours. One major raid in October struck a large field where thousands of refugees had encamped; my friend Zigurds saw some gory sights there afterwards.

During one night raid I left the shelter, thinking the planes were hitting another part of town, and started to take a time exposure of a "Christmas Tree" flare that was slowly descending. Suddenly I heard the ominous whistle of a bomb and scrambled back into the doorway, just as the bomb exploded some 100 m away. During the weeks when Erica was out digging trenches while I stayed at home, I never washed dishes until the evening, not wanting to waste any effort in case a bomb hit the house. But by the time we left Liepāja, only a few windows in our apartment were broken.

There were other signs that the front was near, such as a German tank that appeared a few blocks from our house. I also saw two generals walking along the street. In earlier years, I had occasionally seen a general flit by in a chauffeur-driven car, but never *two*, and never on foot.

Shortly before we left, I received a pathetic letter from my friend Haralds Neimanis (Fig. 8), who was with a Latvian military unit somewhere south of Liepāja, perhaps in Western Poland. He was exhausted from combat, mud, rain, filth, lack of sleep, etc., and sounded very despondent. Little more than a year earlier, during our trip to the Rīga archives, Erica and I had accidentally run into Haralds. He was wearing an elegant uniform that I did not recognize (perhaps of some special Latvian unit), was overjoyed at seeing us, and seemed very happy with his situation. Now he was at the end of his tether. I replied right away but left Liepāja before he could answer. I wonder if he survived the war.

Not being able to foretell the future, we never know when seeing a relative or friend that this is the last time. Later we have regrets. If we knew it beforehand, we might act differently or at least turn sentimental. Perhaps it is just as well that we don't.

Refugee ships were leaving every few days, and in the second week of October, the ban on evacuation of men was suddenly lifted. Only in 1997 did I learn the reason. On 9 Oct the Soviet troops advancing through Lithuania had reached the Baltic coast some 70 km south of Liepāja and thus cut off Courland where the 16. and 18. German armies were massed, with more than half a million German and Latvian troops, 1,000 tanks, and 1,500 planes. Rīga fell on 13 Oct. The German High Command ordered a breakout to Eastern Prussia (Operation Vulture) to start on 17 Oct, and decided to evacuate loyal men of military age rather than let them fall into the hands of the Soviets; these men could be sorted out and drafted in Germany. There was no time to issue entry permits, so all I needed was my clearance slip from the police.

We jumped at the opportunity and packed 4 suitcases and a couple of trunks. (Refugees had a fairly generous baggage allowance, and baggage transport by rail and sea still functioned rather well, 6 months before the capitulation of Germany). Erica had mixed feelings about abandoning our home and our possessions, but I was not bothered at all. I picked out some of my father's business papers; including two pending claims from his last export transactions in 1940. We never collected the $1,100 on these claims, but the ledgers, business license, and bank records were helpful in getting a German pension for my mother in 1956.

TO GERMANY

With about 2,000 other refugees, we left in the evening of 15 Oct 44 on a flea-infested freighter. As the ship—totally blacked out except for a few blue emergency lights—glided out of the harbor, a Soviet air raid started. The detonations of bombs and anti-aircraft shells were an impressive send-off, if not quite equal to a 21-gun salute.

In 1997 I learned that the farewell air raid was the prelude to a major Soviet offensive the next morning. By coincidence or espionage, the Red Army had chosen to attack one day before Operation Vulture, thus thwarting the breakout to East Prussia. The battle raged until 19 Oct, and after a 5-day lull, Soviet forces again attacked. Breakout by land was no longer possible, but when some top German generals suggested evacuation by sea, Hitler allegedly shouted, "Out of the question!" Fortress Courland withstood another 4 Soviet offensives and surrendered only after the capitulation of Germany on 8 May 1945. A major reason for hanging on was that the Germans needed the southern Baltic as training ground for a new class of submarines, the Walter U-Boat, which could travel under water at more than 20 knots, nearly 3 times faster than conventional U-Boats and faster than most convoy escort ships.[29] By the end of the war, 181 of these submarines had been built, but only 6 were operational and had no effect on the war.

It was a good thing we didn't linger in Liepāja because 3 weeks later all draft deferments were canceled, and men were once again forbidden to leave. Moreover, life in Liepāja became

[29] Gerhard L. Weinberg: *A World at Arms*, Cambridge: University Press, 1994, 386–387.

ever more grim in the final months, as I learned in 2003 from the Linkimer Diary.[30] The Red Army noose around the town tightened steadily, air raids became more frequent and heavier, augmented by artillery once the Soviets had advanced within range. German gendarmes conducted almost daily man-hunts, rounding up able-bodied men and women for transport to the Reich. Naturally the troops had priority on the dwindling food supply, causing growing famine among civilians.

---

[30] Kalman Linkimer. *19 Months in a Cellar: How 11 Jews Eluded Hitler's Henchmen. A Diary, 1944–1945.* Translated from Yiddish by Rebecca Margolis, edited by Edward Anders. (Rīga: Museum "Jews in Latvia" and Jewish Community of Rīga, 2008, 116–154; hereafter cited as Linkimer).

8. GERMANY AND
SUDETENLAND: 1944–45

AVING BETTER luck than some other refugee ships that were
sunk by Soviet bombers or mines, we disembarked in
Gdansk (Danzig) the next evening.[31] We boarded a train
that left the following evening, reaching the small Pomeranian
town of Stargard in the afternoon of 18 Oct. There we were
placed in a transient camp—formerly a satellite of the
Ravensbrück concentration camp for women but now assigned
to friendly refugees. It retained many of its original charms,
including lice as well as the ubiquitous fleas. Those of us who
got an invitation from friends in Germany would be allowed to
leave; all others would be sent to the *Warthegau*. We promptly
wrote to Mrs. Fischer—wife of our former roomer—in
Chomutov (Komotau), Sudetenland, who soon confirmed her
standing invitation.

---

[31] I started a diary on leaving home—actually only a concise chronology on a
single 3"x3" piece of paper. I still have it and thus can give exact times for the
principal events in the first 15 months after leaving home. For example, my
first and last encounter with a louse took place on 19 Oct 44 at 4 PM.

But 2 days later, on 21 Oct, I came down with diphtheria. Erica rightly distrusted the camp infirmary and did not rest until she had gotten me into a German auxiliary hospital for diphtheria cases (mainly children under 10), located in a school where the dominant fauna was bedbugs rather than fleas. The staff, two Italian POW doctors—Ezio Bianchi and Aldo Landi—and a few German nurses, took good care of me, and I recovered after 3 weeks. (Thirty-four years later, we had a memorable reunion with Dr. Ezio Bianchi, after Joan tracked him down through the Milan phone book. After the war, he had tried without success to locate Dr. Landi and my Italian POW roommate, Virginio Manfrin, so apparently they did not survive. Bianchi told me at our reunion that the head nurse in Stargard had "some suspicions" about me—presumably my Aryan blood. Fortunately she did not pursue the matter.)

WE BECOME ETHNIC GERMANS

On 11 Nov, when I was discharged from the hospital, Erica bribed our way (probably with Latvian silver coins) into a hotel for a few days. In my Courland naiveté I was about to list myself as a half-Jew on the police registration form, when I suddenly realized that nobody knew me here, so that I could pass for a full-fledged ethnic German if I wanted to. Lack of a proper ID was no longer a problem, because as a refugee I could always claim to have lost mine. Also, my aquiline ID from the Rustin Institute had just gained quasi-official status, having been stamped by a German immigration official in Gdansk.

We spent the next several hours going through our papers and tearing up everything that indicated our non-Aryan background. That included the expired *Gebietskommissar* pass, our precious correspondence with the archives, and pictures of all relatives who looked Jewish. Anybody watching us would have suspected a severe case of dysentery, as we paid frequent visits to the WC down the hall in order to flush down the incriminating shreds.

On 17 Nov at midnight we arrived in Chomutov, spent the night in the station, and then found our way to Mrs. Fischer. She warmly welcomed us, especially after we offered her some of the

5 lb. of Latvian bacon we had brought with us. She then sent us upstairs for a rest after our sleepless night. A few hours later I opened my mother's suitcase that she had left unlocked in the kitchen, and was horrified to find a little brown book at the very top: *a prayer book for Jewish women, in German!* Rather out of place for an ethnic German.

I shall never know whether Mrs. Fischer or her two daughters—all rather nosy—had looked inside our suitcases. In any case, they never said anything to the authorities about our non-Aryan background. When we had worn out our welcome (as soon as the bacon was gone), we moved into a hotel and applied to the Nazi Social Welfare organization (*NSV*) for a room. At first they regarded us as Latvians and said we should be in a camp, but when Erica (with just the right degree of indignation) protested our ethnic German status, the woman official yielded, despite the suspicious entry in Erica's ID card: "~~Volksdeutsche~~ *Lettland*". She began to dictate a letter to a prospective landlady, referring to Erica as "*Volksgenossin* (fellow German) Erika Alperowitz". Hearing this, Erica smiled at me triumphantly. I cringed, but fortunately the woman had not been looking at Erica that moment.

On 9 Dec we moved into our room, which was located in a 4-flat building in the nicest part of Chomutov. Our landlady lived in another town and showed up only 1 or 2 days a month. Despite the housing shortage caused by millions of bombed-out refugees, she apparently had enough "pull" to keep two apartments, except for the token concession of renting one room. Even that room was kept "under the table" until sufficiently civilized tenants showed up. Luckily we qualified.

Some 800,000 tons of bombs (equivalent to ~50 Hiroshima-sized atomic bombs) had fallen on Germany by late 1944, but German society still functioned—at the expense of the occupied countries, of course. Airplane production actually *peaked* in the last months of 1944! Food rations were more generous than in Latvia and were readily available in stores. Price controls functioned despite the tremendously inflated money supply, and there was only a minor black market in scarce items such as fruit. Restaurant meals were affordable in terms of price and ration coupons. As *Volksdeutsche* refugees, we even got free unfinished furniture for our room, such as beds (albeit with straw sacks for mattresses), a stove, etc., as well as ration cards for a pair of shoes and a few other items. We subsisted mainly by selling or bartering our belongings, as we had been doing for some time.

I was amazed occasionally to see a few soldiers in British uniforms on the street—unarmed but without guards, walking proudly with heads held high. They were British POWs from Cyprus, which was still a British colony at that time. In their smart, neatly pressed uniforms they looked more elegant than the German soldiers who were clearly showing the wear and tear of 5+ years of war, to say nothing of the pathetic, rag-clad Soviet POWs we had seen in Latvia. One could not ask for a more vivid illustration of the Geneva Convention, which the Nazis applied to POWs from Western but not Eastern countries.

About 100,000 Latvian refugees were now in Germany or German-occupied territory. One day a middle-aged woman approached Erica on the street and addressed her in Latvian, explaining, "You have a Latvian face". We took that as a high compliment. The woman shared our dislike of the Soviets, but when Erica tried to cheer her shortly before the end of the war with the rumor that American tanks had been sighted only 100 km away, she showed her true colors by replying, "Yes, but who sat in those tanks? Jews and Negroes!"

Saved by a Heart Condition

A week after we had moved in, the Battle of the Bulge (aka Ardennes offensive) started. We had no radio and got only the German side of the story, which seemed rather unsettling. But on 20 Dec, just as the tide turned, I fell ill with a severe heart condition (myocarditis), a not uncommon aftereffect of diphtheria in adults. That's why the Italian doctors in Stargard had listened to my heart several times a day. At first Dr. Lachnit-Irzing, MD daughter of the Irzing family downstairs, tried to take care of me but 2 weeks later she decided I had to be hospitalized. During my second morning in the ward I heard that the nuns had been looking for an English-speaking person during the night, to speak to a dying British POW. He was dead by morning and I greatly regretted having slept through the call.

Germany was only 3–4 months away from final collapse, but the care was good, as was the food. Erica, eager to do something for me, had walked around town until she spotted some fruit trees, and then bartered a Latvian silver coin for a few pears.

My two roommates were loyal Nazis. One, a middle-aged paperhanger, occasionally ranted about the allied "terror bombers", vowing to string up the pilots on the nearest tree if he caught any. Belying the cliché that Nazis were conformists, he had a very original way of administering *digitalis* suppositories: he cut them up into little pieces and swallowed them with his coffee. Perhaps his anatomy was so symmetrical that it did not make any difference. Anyhow, he did not live to see the end of the war. Like several of our previous roommates, he was wheeled out into a private room where he died during the night.

I was still in the hospital on 13 Feb 1945 when the great Royal Air Force raid on Dresden took place. An alert sounded in the evening and we all went into the cellar. [There were two waves of attack, by 244 bombers at 10:14 PM and 529 bombers at 1:14 AM. The first, being smaller and "less successful" has completely faded from my memory; my recollections seem to match the second one.] Realizing before long that the bombers had another target that night, several of us went out on the street and saw countless white flashes on the northern horizon in the direction of Dresden, 60 km away on the other side of the *Erzgebirge* mountains. Gradually the white flashes were superseded by a steady orange glow, rising higher and higher in the sky. Evidently the city was on fire. It struck all of us that countless people were perishing in the flames. I do not recall hearing any sound, perhaps there was a distant rumble, but the orange glow alone was spooky enough.

A debate has raged ever since whether this raid was a war crime. Dresden, with a pre-war population of 642,000, was a large city and an important road and railroad junction, but it had little military industry and was packed with some 200,000 refugees from the east. Raids against major railroad junctions had been requested by the Soviets, in view of intercepted German plans to shift half a million troops from Italy, Norway, etc. to the Eastern Front. Allied bombers had long ago given up precision bombing in favor of carpet-bombing from high altitude, which minimized aircraft losses but caused high casualties among civilians. Some 25,000–35,000 people, including many Latvian refugees, were killed in Dresden that night, half the buildings were totally destroyed, and some 30% damaged. In this 6th year of a very bloody war such casualty figures no longer caused much of a shock, especially as it was the Germans who had started the bombing of civilians in 1939–41 (Warsaw, Rotterdam, Coventry, London, etc.). Nonetheless, such high casualties in a city with few military targets caused second thoughts and even discomfort in Washington and London.[32]

I was discharged as "improved" from the county hospital on 3 March, but was allowed to get up only 6 hours a day and remained mostly bedridden for months afterwards. Though my illness seemed a calamity at the time, it saved me from worse troubles. There were few 18-year-olds still out of uniform at that stage of the war, but for some unknown reason, the German Army never came after me. Perhaps they did not know of my existence although we had dutifully registered with the police, or they were not sure of the draft liability of ethnic Germans from Latvia. But a man at the State Employment Office was determined to put me in uniform nonetheless. The most he was empowered to do was to assign me to a paramilitary unit (*Werkschutz*) whose job was to guard Soviet POWs and to squeeze the last ounce of work out of them, by beatings if necessary. Many of these slave drivers were killed by their victims at the end of the war, and so I was lucky to be able to decline the numerous summonses I received in the hospital. But as soon as I was discharged, my "friend" at the Employment Office sent me to his official doctor, who, after watching my pulse rise to 200 upon mild exercise, certified me as disabled until 15 May 1945. Conveniently, the war ended on 8 May 1945.

End of the "Thousand-Year Reich"

Certainly until February or March 1945, many Germans still believed in eventual victory. The Nazis had lost only small border areas of the German heartland, still held Northern Italy, Norway, Denmark, and Holland, and were now putting their hopes into fearsome new weapons that would turn the tide. The V1 buzz bombs and V2 rockets of the summer of 1944 were to be followed by other "V-weapons" (*Vergeltungswaffen* = retaliatory

---

[32] W. F. Craven and J. L. Cate, *The Army Air Forces in World War II. Vol. 3, Europe: Argument to V-E Day.* (Chicago: Univ. Chicago Press, 1951).

weapons), for which Minister of Propaganda Goebbels had raised high hopes by claiming that a demonstration had "made the blood freeze in my veins". The papers and radio were full of stories how Frederick the Great of Prussia had kept on fighting during the darkest days of the Seven-Years' War (1756–63) and eventually prevailed over the 20-fold greater forces of Austria, Russia, and France. Hitler himself had said earlier: "The German Empire in WWI had stopped at five minutes to twelve. I have always, on principle, continued until a quarter past twelve." Although air raids had severely damaged many German cities, production of aircraft and other weapons actually peaked in August to December 1944, and the Battle of the Bulge suggested that the Wehrmacht had not lost its punch. For people unwilling to contemplate German defeat, there were plenty of straws to grasp.

Nighttime air alerts occurred almost weekly in March and April, causing us and our neighbors to gather in the basement for an hour or two. One of these raids hit the large steel mill in Chomutov, allegedly killing 500 people, but the others were aimed at other cities. One night in the shelter people began to quiz Erica what the Russians were like, realizing that we had spent a year under Stalin. Hoping to gain status among these well-to-do burghers, Erica spun a yarn about a Russian general who saw our apartment, fell in love with it and wanted it badly, but then left with a long face when she refused to let him have it. Her audience wrongly concluded that the Russians couldn't be so bad after all, if they so readily took no for an answer. I cringed once again.

By April, most of our neighbors realized that Hitler's "Thousand-Year Reich" was nearing its end. The Irzing family on the ground floor (whose MD daughter had taken care of me before my hospitalization) became quite outspoken, admitting that they were now listening to the BBC (although the death penalty for this offense was still on the books), and worried what the Allies would do to those Germans who belonged to the Nazi Party. Seeking to reassure them, I said I, too, had just started listening to the BBC, and heard that in some small town, the British had appointed a man as mayor although he had been a

Nazi Party member. "Oh, they reported that a few weeks ago", said our neighbor, implying that we both had been listening to the BBC longer than we had admitted. But I didn't worry about them reporting me, as they now asked me for a favor. They had been custodians of the building's swastika flag, which they hoisted on holidays. Now they wanted to dispose of the flag before Allied troops arrived, but were afraid to do so in their ground-floor apartment where passers-by could look in. Was it OK for them to come up and burn the flag in our stove? I consented without unseemly enthusiasm, and watched the process with profound, if hidden, glee.

A few times I went for walks with Dagmar Knapp, a high school teacher's daughter I had met in the hospital. She knew that the war was lost and said, "I expect that the Allies will do to us what we did to the Jews". Once again I was reminded that Germans come in all shadings.

Signs of the impending collapse began to mount. For a day or two, an endless column of people shuffled westward past our house: mainly civilian refugees, interspersed with occasional soldiers (AWOL?) and a few concentration camp prisoners in striped garb. I still remember the haunted, half-crazed look of one of them, who moved his limbs jerkily like a robot. In the final months of the war, hundreds of thousands of such prisoners had been driven westward before the advancing Soviets, under such inhumane conditions that most of them died.

For once, Erica showed admirable presence of mind on the morning of 1 May 45, when a tearful woman told her that "the *Führer* has fallen in combat in Berlin". Erica promptly covered her mouth to hide her grin, and let out an ambiguous gasp. She thought she could let down her guard a week later, just after Germany's unconditional surrender had been announced, but when she ran into an old woman on the street, the following dialogue ensued:

W.:   What is all this commotion about?
E.:   The war is over.
W.:   Great, so we have won!
E.:   No, we lost.

W.: How dare you spread such lies? I'll report you to the Gestapo!

In late April, Chomutov looked like a good place to await the Western Allies. US troops had already occupied Cheb (Eger) in westernmost Sudetenland, 90 km away, while the Soviets were still hundreds of kilometers to the East. We didn't know about the Yalta agreement, however, which specified demarcation lines in advance rather than letting the race go to the swiftest. Thus we watched with growing apprehension as the Soviets advanced westward, while the Americans seemed to be marking time, first at Cheb and then, reportedly, at Karlovy Vary (Karlsbad), only 45 km away.

OVERTAKEN BY THE RED ARMY

When Germany capitulated on May 8, only a few areas still were under her control, including Courland, where we came from, and western Czechoslovakia, where we were. Belatedly, we realized that the mountain was not coming to Mohammed, and that we would have to move westward. We and the Irzings packed our essentials and rushed to the railroad station where Erica talked our way onto a Red Cross train that was repatriating 200 French officers and several political prisoners from East Germany to the West, including the Crown Prince of Montenegro, the last Lithuanian Prime Minister, a Belgian priest, etc. That evening the train pulled out of the station 6 hours before the Soviets entered the town from the other side.

The train traveled stop-and-go the next day, spending hours at various stations. At one of them an SS officer in full regalia paced the platform, chillingly asserting Nazi power in this last strip of no-man's-land. The next morning (10 May) all civilians were bumped from the train, and so we walked the last 10 kilometers to Karlovy Vary, carrying our suitcases. The Irzings had friends who provided shelter for us all (we got the kitchen), and then we strolled through town in search of the American troops alleged to be there. After spotting a US army jeep at 6 PM, we retired with a feeling of immense relief.

A rude shock awaited us the next morning. As we walked down the stairs, a woman stopped us and said: "Hide your watches and rings—the town is full of Russians". Unbeknownst to us, the Allies had decided that the river Ohře (Eger) flowing through Karlovy Vary was to be the demarcation line between US and Soviet forces. We were on the wrong (east) bank of the Ohře; the US jeep we had seen the day before was merely taking a ride through the still unoccupied Soviet sector.

We had missed freedom by less than a kilometer. However, on that first morning pedestrian traffic still moved unimpeded, so we went to US headquarters in the Hotel Richmond and told an officer who we were. He asked us to go back to our kitchen and return in a few days "after the US has established control". But that time never came; within a day the token US force had withdrawn some tens of kilometers westward. Once again we were in Stalin's clutches.

We briefly returned to Chomutov on 20 May to retrieve some of our abandoned belongings. Here, out of sight of Americans, the Soviet soldiers had been their usual selves. A couple of women on our block had been raped, as were many others in town. Some Soviet soldiers had broken into our apartment and helped themselves to our landlady's belongings. With evident skill they had slit our suitcase open by a C-shaped bayonet cut in the lid, but found only my chemicals collection. Disappointed, they took only a few things from our room: mainly some girls' pictures from my photo album, presumably for bragging back home.

My heart condition, aggravated by the march to Karlovy Vary, enabled us to stall for time and put off repatriation to Latvia. (There a bad fate would have awaited us. The Soviets took the attitude that any Jew who survived Hitler's concentration camps must have collaborated with the Nazis and deserved at least 10 years in the Gulag; I heard of many such cases over the years. It is not hard to guess how they would have looked upon us who had *not* been in concentration camps.) Erica, with her talent for striking up conversations with strangers, had met a few Soviet MDs from a military hospital in the Hotel Imperial, and so charmed them with her fluent Russian that they kept supplying us with food, including our first tuna (from the US). Indeed, she soon turned them into a source of income, by buying costume jewelry from an obscure tourist shop in town and selling it to the Soviets at a steep markup. At one point, Erica was quizzed by the local NKVD in the Villa Loretta, but deftly talked her way out of this predicament.

Karlovy Vary was a pretty little town full of hotels and shops that had flourished for centuries from people's belief in the wondrous curative powers of the local hot springs—essentially a dilute solution of sodium bicarbonate (baking soda). It certainly was an excellent remedy for heartburn, and an agreeable placebo for myriad other ailments. Our room in a downscale guest house looked out on the biggest and hottest outlet, a gusher of 73°C called *Sprudel* (Vřídlo). But there were other outlets along the promenade ranging all the way down to a temperate 40°C, each with its own name implying distinctive medical effects. The many doctors in town would prescribe a customized treatment for each patient: while strolling along the promenade for x minutes, slowly drink a cup from a particular outlet, then go to your hotel and lie down for half an hour. Repeat this hocus-pocus 3 times a day. The hot springs were quite prolific, enabling Karlovy Vary to offer baths in this miraculous water, administered in a number of bath houses ranging from the sumptuous Imperial Baths (formerly patronized by Austrian emperors) to more modest establishments.

The processions of jewel- and fur-bedecked matrons that used to stroll along the promenade were gone by 1945, and except for some luxury hotels converted to military hospitals, hotels were filled with refugees and other ordinary folk. Red Army soldiers showed little interest in the internal or external uses of Karlovy Vary waters.

Karlovy Vary is situated in a narrow river valley surrounded by wooded hills. For the benefit of people "taking the waters" there were many gently graded paths with benches. I had suffered a relapse from the exertions of getting to Karlovy Vary, but as my condition improved, I began to take walks in the hills and eventually made it to the top. I climbed the lookout tower and was overwhelmed by the sight of the town in the valley, spread out like a toy village. Having grown up in flat Latvia and never flown in a plane, I had never seen such a sight. I took a few pictures then and again 50 years later when Joan and I visited the same spot.

The Czechs had been badly treated by the Nazis: a German librarian in Chomutov proudly told me in 1944 how the local Czechs were shipped off in *open coal cars* to the interior of the country. Now the Czechs retaliated. Germans were required to wear white armbands and got food rations only 50% those of Czechs and Slovaks. (Jews and Austrians, despite their vastly different status in the Third Reich, both got 75%). In August or September the Czechs began to expel Sudeten Germans across the border with little more than the clothes on their backs. The expulsions continued until early 1946 and became quite brutal at times, with thousands of Germans perishing.

I did not yet know that Oskar Schindler ("Schindler's List") was a Sudeten German, but I had met enough decent Germans to be greatly troubled by such collective punishment. True, there were Nazis among them. The man in whose kitchen we slept after arrival in Karlovy Vary was very depressed by Germany's defeat, and said: "I have studied the matter very thoroughly, and know that it's the fault of international Jewry." Another said after Roosevelt's death on 12 Apr 45 of a cerebral hemorrhage, "I wish the whole US Army had died of a cerebral hemorrhage".

GETTING TO THE WEST

By late September, our situation had become precarious. US and Soviet troops soon were to leave Czechoslovakia, and the Soviets were beginning to round up their citizens. My medical excuse was wearing thin, especially since Erica's Soviet friends offered to take us along on their hospital train. In our incredible naiveté we went to Prague and inquired at the Swiss embassy whether they would let us into their country. The lady we spoke to was exquisitely polite, asked us how we expected to support ourselves, and then explained that Switzerland was *überfremdet* (had too many foreigners). It was only 46 years later that we were welcome to live in Switzerland.

Courland Jews have a reputation of being honest but naïve and provincial, and we certainly fit that stereotype. I am not sure what would have become of us if worldlier people had not given us some good advice. The Iron Curtain, though tight across Germany, had remained porous in Czechoslovakia, in anticipation of the withdrawal of occupation forces. A Romanian Jewish woman in Karlovy Vary told us that we could get out easily by taking a train from Karlovy Vary to the nearest town in the US Zone, Mariánske Lázňe (Marienbad), 43 km away. We did so on 8 Oct 1945 and easily passed the Soviet, Czech, and American passport controls, having taken the precaution of sitting in the farthest corner of the converted freight car, where the soldiers couldn't easily approach us within reading distance. My travel document, now that the Rustin Institute's eagle had become a liability, was a long-expired Latvian school ID card. To the Soviet and American soldiers, Latvian and Czech must have looked the same, having similar diacritics. I shall never know what it looked like to the Czech policeman, who also waved us on.

Once in Mariánske Lázňe, we went to the US commandant's office and explained our wish to go West. But the officer said that he could do nothing for us as we lived in Karlovy Vary and were not under his jurisdiction. We left with long faces, but the interpreter, a German civilian, followed us into the hall and told us what to do. "Check into a hotel and register with the police. Then you come under the standing rule of the US Military Government that DPs who do not want to go back to their homeland are shipped off to West Germany." He had a hammer-and-sickle lapel pin indicating that he was a communist, but apparently his sympathy for us trumped his loyalty to the USSR. We took his advice, packed our belongings, returned to Mariánske Lázňe on 14 Oct, and followed his procedure. On 17 Oct we went to the appointed place at 8.00 and waited for the US Army truck that was to take us to a transient camp in Plzeň (Pilsen), for transport to Germany. Now our lives were once again saved by a fluke.

Hours went by with no sign of the truck. More refugees (mainly German) had gathered behind us in an orderly queue, and we eventually noticed that all had name tags tied to their luggage. Thinking this a good idea, I hurried off to a stationery store, only to discover that the Czech shopkeeper was in no mood to sell anything to a German-speaking person. I was brusquely turned down at several other stores before I finally got the tags. When I got back at 12, I found that a large US Army trailer truck had arrived and had nearly finished loading the refugees and their luggage. We had lost our place in line and had to sit in the very back of the truck rather than the very front.

On the 2-lane road to Plzeň, I stood up in the back of the open trailer, enjoying the breeze in my face. Suddenly an overhanging branch from a roadside tree struck my forehead, and I quickly sat down. A woman looked at me and screamed, because blood was pouring down my face from a deep gash in my scalp. There was no time for first aid, because the speeding truck skidded, hit the roadside trees, and overturned. I felt myself flying through the air and landed in the soft grass without further injuries. Most other people were similarly unhurt; only 4 or 5 in the very front of the truck were killed. That's exactly where we would have been sitting if the Czech shopkeepers had not given me such a hard time about the tags.

An ambulance arrived and took me and two more severely injured people to a Czech hospital. The Czech medic became noticeably friendlier after ascertaining that I was not German, but presumably withheld Class A treatment when I answered "no" to his question, whether Latvians were a Slavic people. Anyhow, they stitched the 10-cm gash in my scalp. Later I heard that the other two people had died. The driver survived.

The camp gave us our first exposure to some really crooked Jews from Poland, Hungary, etc. A woman accosted us at the camp office (where we had just received a vague answer to our question when we would be shipped off to Germany) and told us that for 500 marks, she could arrange a "left" (illegal) way for us to be sent to Bavaria. When we did not flinch, she repeated the offer, but deftly raised the price to 5,000. By then I had gotten my defenses up and said that we would rather wait for the legal way. "There is no such thing", she replied, "everything here is done the left way".

But the very next evening, we were put on a train to Germany. The following day, 20 Oct, we crossed the border of US-occupied Bavaria. At last we felt safe! For the first time since

17 June 1940, we were no longer afraid of the knock on the door—the most basic difference between a police state and a free country.

Yet it would be wrong to think that I spent the 5 war years in a constant state of terror. Though deeply scarred by the loss of 25 relatives, we had experienced little physical suffering and were nearly untouched by military action. We had lived through numerous air raids by the four major powers, but remained unhurt, suffering no greater harm than some broken windows. Like most people—especially teenagers—in similar situations, I had tuned out the constant danger, and became engrossed in the trivia of everyday life.

I do not think the war had much of an effect on my personality. Most of my faults—hypersensitivity, impatience, short temper—I had abundantly before the war. One lesson I learned, though, is not to make invidious generalizations about any group but to judge people as individuals. I met enough decent, brave, and noble Germans and Latvians during the war to become immunized against prejudice. Another lesson was to accept mortality and not fear death.

9. MUNICH: 1945–1949

ON 21 OCTOBER we reached Munich and were assigned to the DP camp *Föhrenwald* near Wolfratshausen, a former workers' dormitory some 30 km south of Munich. These camps were run by UNRRA (United Nations Relief and Rehabilitation Administration). Housing was not bad as camps go; Erica and I had a room to ourselves, sharing a communal bathroom down the hall with a dozen other people. Meals were provided in a large mess hall.

I got a job as a draftsman at the camp office, receiving a can of canned goods per day in lieu of salary. That was welcome as the food in the camp was skimpy and mediocre, due to rampant theft by the kitchen staff as I later discovered. I asked a young UNRRA official, Marion van Binsbergen,[33] how I might complete my last 3 years of high school, and she referred me to the UNRRA University that was being organized by DPs (Displaced Persons) in the *Deutsches Museum* in Munich, a huge museum of science and technology. During the war the exhibits had been removed to make room for offices and a dormitory for Soviet

---

[33] I met her again in Bern 53 years later and learned only then that she had been active in the Dutch Resistance and had saved, or tried to save, 150 Jews. Her married name is Pritchard and she lives in Vershire, VT.

slave laborers. Though the building was considerably damaged during a 1944 air raid, UNRRA used parts for a DP transient camp and assigned another part to the UNRRA University.

THE UNRRA UNIVERSITY

I learned that though the UNRRA University did not plan to establish a high school, it had started a 6-week refresher course for people who had lost their high school diplomas. Anyone who passed oral examinations in 9 subjects at the end of the course would receive a certificate qualifying him for admission to the UNRRA University.

Although I had not gotten very far with the Rustin home study program, it had at least kept me from forgetting what I knew. I had missed the first two weeks of the refresher course but promptly enrolled on ~16 Nov, got up at 5 every morning to take the train to Munich, and returned around 8 PM. About a week later Erica and I moved to Munich and got a furnished room.

The lecture rooms at the university had no heat and most of their windows were broken, but we kept our overcoats and gloves on in the December cold without complaining. All of us— some 200 DPs—were glad at this chance to resume our education after several years as prisoners, slave laborers, refugees, or outcasts. Just before Christmas I passed the exams, got my certificate, and enrolled as a student at the UNRRA University when classes started on 16 Jan 1946. But that 3-year gap in my education repeatedly troubled me later in life.

The chemistry professor Michael Samygin, a young Russian, hired me as a laboratory assistant and at the end of January 1946 I began to set up a qualitative analysis laboratory. I put my heart and soul into that task for several months, often neglecting my classes, but then had the satisfaction of seeing the lab full of students even before the end of the semester.

Faculty and students at the UNRRA University were a motley mix of Eastern Europeans: Poles, Ukrainians, Russians, Yugoslavs, Latvians, Lithuanians, Estonians, etc. Many were genuine "displaced persons" whom the Nazis had persecuted but there also were others whom they had treated as loyal if second-class allies. Political screening was supposed to filter out real Nazi collaborators, but was less than 100% efficient.

The faculty was of variable quality, ranging from first- to third-rate. The university had hired all the warm bodies it could find in the US Zone, but still had major gaps in several fields. Thus, for lack of chemistry professors we chemistry students were told to take several irrelevant subjects such as physical geography.

Most of us arrived with ethnic prejudices but gradually overcame them as we got to know individuals from other nations. Much the same process took place every year in the International House in New York where I lived 1949–51. There foreign students from dozens of countries lived under the same roof with American students, building friendships and often developing a life-long commitment to the House motto "That Brotherhood May Prevail".

The Jewish students at the UNRRA University remained aloof, however. Having experienced murders and savage persecutions by some members of certain nations, they did not want to have anything to do with these nations, formed their own student organization and kept to themselves. Early on, a Jewish student whom I had gotten to know urged me to join the Jewish student organization, comprised mainly of Polish Jews. But as soon as I did I was summoned before their "Court of Honor". There I was asked to prove that I was Jewish. Having destroyed all such evidence in 1944, I showed them the documents I had received after the end of the war, but that did not satisfy them, and the president threw a challenge at me: "You claim to be Alperovitch but how do I know that your name last year was not Göring?" (Strange how Göring kept intruding in my life; in 1943 I was suspected of being under his protection.) I pulled out my highschool ID from 1940, showing my picture at age 14 and my name as "Alperovičs". With visible chagrin the president accepted my claim. Ironically, a few months later I was elected to the same Court of Honor. But the incident had not exactly increased my eagerness to associate with this organization.

Soon Erica had a similar experience. The Jewish Central Committee in Munich, which among other things certified the Jewishness of DPs to make them eligible for larger food rations and preferences in housing, had gotten suspicious of my mother's bonas fides and summoned her before a committee of rabbis and other experts. My mother made good use of her fluent Yiddish and her acting talents to make the committee look like fools, but she overheard one member whisper to the other, "perhaps her *mother* was not Jewish". It's a good thing there was no similar skeptic whispering into SS-*Untersturmführer* Kügler's ear in July 1941 when Erica tried to convince him that she was German.

Two months later, when the University of Munich opened, I enrolled there, too, in order to piece together a halfway sensible program from the fragmentary offerings of the two schools. It was not easy to get an education at the University of Munich at that time. The faculty had been decimated by death, emigration, or dismissal for Nazi party membership. Buildings had been destroyed or damaged by air raids, with the result that lectures were held in unheated class rooms at widely scattered locations, connected by a streetcar system of legendary inadequacy. Textbooks were generally unavailable. Laboratories, when finally repaired, had waiting lists of several years.

Of my teachers at U. Munich, Klaus Clusius made the greatest impression upon me. He was a brilliant lecturer who turned his physical chemistry course into an exciting experience. I was also very impressed by Rolf Huisgen's stereochemistry course, though parts of it were over my head because I had not yet taken the basic organic chemistry course.

The End of the UNRRA University

But soon other activities encroached on my studies—and, as discussed later in this chapter, on my prospects of emigrating to the US. In early 1947 UNRRA suddenly closed the University in mid-semester, ostensibly for financial reasons.[34] Students were

---

[34] This story is also told by Mark Wyman in: *DPs: Europe's Displaced Persons, 1945–1951*, (Ithaca: Cornell Univ. Press, 1998). The closing was officially explained in *UNRRA Team News* "as part of the Munich community's fuel conservation program".

locked out of the building but then gathered in a lecture
another wing. Teams of laborers led by an UNRR/
entered to dismantle our laboratories. As a laboratory assistant ı
had a faculty pass to the library, got into the building and
rushed up to "my" lab, where the goons had just started to pack
the chemicals into boxes. I protested to the UNRRA official who
was arrogant and unmoved until the door opened and hundreds
of students, led by some tall, husky fellows, poured in. Somehow
they had found out what was going on and had pushed their
way past the guards into the building.

Pinned to a lab bench by the crowd, the UNRRA man
suddenly became very conciliatory and agreed to retreat with his
goons, leaving everything behind. We kept guarding the lab for
several more days and then moved everything to the building of
the "Free Ukrainian University", which had been established in
another part of town. There our students were able to finish the
semester. After that at least the better students succeeded in
getting into German universities.

Together with another half-dozen young idealists from the
university's student organization, I worked nearly full-time for a
year, unsuccessfully trying to revive what we regarded as a
pioneering experiment in international education. Our president
was **Valerius Michelson** from St. Petersburg, a brilliant student
of architecture.

Born in 1916, he was drafted into the Red Army at the start of the
war and was taken prisoner in the first few months, when the
Germans captured several million Soviet soldiers. Expecting early
victory the Nazis wanted to get rid of these "subhuman" Slavs as
quickly as possible, using any means available. In the bitterly cold
winter 1941/42 Val and his comrades did forced labor during the
day, and at night were housed in a bombed out factory without roof
or windows. The POWs slept in a heap, every morning pushing
aside the top layer of frozen corpses. Val escaped, and thanks to
his fluent German was able to subsist somehow in Nazi Germany.
(He had learned German as a child in Estonia where his father had
fled to during the October 1917 revolution, only to be lured back to
his death after Lenin announced his New Economic Policy in 1921).
After the end of WWII the Western Allies permitted non-Soviet DPs
refusing to return to their home countries to stay in the West. But for
a number of months they forcibly repatriated Soviet DPs, many of
whom committed suicide. Val therefore changed his biography,

pretending that he had never lived in the USSR. He married an Estonian widow and emigrated to the US in 1950, becoming a very successful architect in St. Paul, MN.

We found a few sympathizers among German intellectuals, including the young journalist **Dr. Hildegard Brücher**, who later became a leading politician in the FDP (Free Democratic Party). But none had sufficient influence to help us realize our plans. At last we somehow connected with a bizarre character: a 60-ish "Professor" **Lüdke** who had founded an organization "Brotherhood of the Cross *Pro Una Sancta Ecclesia*", whose goal was to reunify all Christian churches—on the terms of the Catholic Church. It is not clear whether this organization had any members other than Lüdke and his deputy, the "Frenchman" **Cusé-Cerf** (whom Lüdke after their breakup called an Alsatian). Lüdke thought that a university belonging to Pro Una Sancta Ecclesia would greatly enhance his status, and he particularly coveted the founding charter of the University, signed in 1946 by Lt. Gen. Lucien K. Truscott, commander of the US Third Army. Lüdke drafted bizarre statutes for the university, according to which the university was entirely responsible for financing whereas he would provide the name and oppressive control.

Lüdke was a fanatical, simple-minded windbag and a consummate namedropper, but although people soon saw through him, the archconservative Catholics who are a major force in Bavaria could not easily dismiss an organization with such laudable goals. Thus he was able to take us to meetings with influential people such as the Education Minister A. A. Hundhammer in Munich and the Prince of Thurn-und-Taxis in Regensburg. The prince was very rich, as his family had owned the postal monopoly for much of Germany in centuries past, and Lüdke hoped that he would donate one of his palaces and some cash for the cause. But of course it came to naught. Apart from his earthly connections he also had excellent contact with the heavens, always knowing which member of the Trinity to credit for an idea or a favorable development. If we rang his doorbell at a particularly auspicious moment when he had some news to share, it was the Holy Ghost that had sent us to him. At other times it was Jesus Christ or the Virgin Mary.

I might have continued to work for this lost cause had I not, in April 1948, finally obtained space in the Qualitative Analysis laboratory of the University of Munich. The program (26 unknowns and 10 inorganic preparations) was much too large and time-consuming by current standards; the lab was open about 10 hours/day and practically became our home where we spent 20–40 hrs/week. However, I enjoyed it and learned a great deal of chemistry while spending many hours in the library looking up new analytical tests that could be used as shortcuts. After finishing the course in record time, I was appointed *famulus* (teaching assistant); an honor offered to only 1–2% of the students and hardly ever a foreigner.

LIFE IN MUNICH

In the first few years after the war, Germany was the poorhouse of Europe. Much of the housing had been destroyed or badly damaged by Allied bombers. The eastern German provinces had been seized by Poland, Czechoslovakia, and the USSR, which expelled some 12 million Germans who now poured into a shrunken Germany. Food rations were very skimpy, as Germany no longer was able to rob the occupied countries. Much of Europe had been badly damaged during the war, and such relief as came from overseas went primarily to the victim countries, not to Germany.

Room and Board

Munich had not been as badly hit as many other cities, but living conditions, though heavenly compared to concentration camps, were not quite up to US standards of 2010. We had one bedroom in the 2-bedroom apartment of the Nazi couple Rädler, who eventually began to complain that they had to share their bedroom with their pre-teen daughter (presumably inhibiting their sex life, which was light punishment for an ex-Nazi). But they kept exclusive use of the bathroom whereas we had only the shared washbasin in the hall, next to the shared WC. We took our baths at a public bath house 2 miles away, where the water was hot but the wait was 2 hours.

The windowpanes of our room had been broken in some air raid long ago. The outer ones had been replaced with translucent plastic reinforced with wire mesh, about as clear as wax paper. The inner panes had been replaced with brown cardboard, nicely color-coordinated with one of our suitcases.

Our food rations were a bit larger than those for Germans, but still inadequate. Restaurants also required ration coupons, but the only way to come out ahead in protein was to order dishes with a high "yuck" score, such as lung stew or blood porridge. Having become accustomed to such fare during the war we did not gag.

DPs would get room and board while living in camps, but once they moved out, they were on their own, "integrated into the German economy". However, DPs who were only briefly away from camp were entitled to a generous ration of canned goods, far exceeding the skimpy amounts of cooked food that the kitchen delivered to the people in the camp. Apparently the Law of Conservation of Matter did not apply to food passing through the camp kitchen. Erica, though living with me in Munich, had maintained her camp registration and occasionally went there by train on Sundays to pick up her rations. That was a welcome supplement until we started to get food parcels from the US and Canada.

Even more welcome were the few packs of American cigarettes that we got with the camp rations or in lieu of pay at the UNRRA University. Hitler had financed his war by printing lots of paper money, relying on the fabled discipline of the German people to keep prices stable. The Allies had brought in plenty of their own "occupation marks", so the country now was awash in paper money. Amazingly, price discipline still held for food rations and the meager selection of goods available in stores and restaurants, as well as for rent, utilities, services, etc. Everything else had to be bought on the black market. DPs, especially Polish Jews, ran a thriving black market on some of the main squares and streets in the center of town. American cigarettes—from DP camps and American GIs—were the principal currency. The price of several weeks' wages per pack remained stable despite the continuing influx, as some were withdrawn from circulation by smoking. Only MPs (military police) but not German police were permitted to arrest DPs, which ensured near-immunity for the black marketers.

Fortunately we began to receive some food parcels from overseas. CARE (Cooperative for American Relief to Europe) had obtained large amounts of surplus canned food from the US Army, much of it in waterproof, waxed cartons labeled "10 Men– 1 Day". CARE offered to deliver them anywhere in Europe for only the shipping cost of $10. GIs had grumbled about these rations but to us everything was new and delicious: powdered orange juice, instant coffee, chocolate bars, crackers, as well as canned goods such as cheese, powdered eggs, hamburgers, vegetables, etc.

A story that circulated among Jewish DPs was that one of them received a letter from his uncle in the US: "...I hear that many DPs sell on the black market some of the canned goods that their relatives send them. That is strictly illegal, and I urge you most emphatically *never* to sell any of the canned goods I send you." When the nephew got the next parcel, he was pleased by the variety of foods but was puzzled by an unlabeled can. When he opened it he found $1,000 inside.

Transportation; A Night in Jail

Munich is a large city, which at that time depended entirely on streetcars for transportation. They were always overcrowded, slow, and late, and as the university departments were scattered throughout the city, commutes from one class to another usually took the better part of an hour. Things got worse during coal shortages that lasted for months at a time. Electricity for homes and streetcars was turned off for several hours in mid-morning and afternoon, keeping it on at noon only long enough for people to get home for their big meal of the day and then rush back to work while the streetcars were still running.

Once in July or August 1946 the streetcar caused me to spend a night in jail. Heading home from classes I joined a crowd waiting for the streetcar, but by the time I had gotten on the step the car was packed and the people inside did not want to squeeze any more tightly to let me in. At that time the rule was that that the streetcar did not move as long as people stood on the step, so the driver and I began a game of chicken. After a couple of minutes a boy of perhaps 18 began to push his way toward the exit. Thinking that he had wanted to get off at the next stop anyway, I stepped aside. But as soon as he had gotten off, he began to hit me with a blackjack, giving me a black eye. I fought back and am not sure how the brawl would have ended if a police car had not arrived.

They took both of us to Police HQ, where we were booked. Once the police discovered that I was a DP they notified the MP (military police), which took me to their station. There I was ushered into a long, narrow cell where 2 Jewish DPs were comfortably stretched out on bunks with their shoes off, airing their fragrant socks. We introduced ourselves, and both my cellmates proclaimed their utter and complete innocence. Two or three MPs were seated in the guardroom from where they could observe us through the door grating. Soon one of them got up, entered our cell asking, "Hey, when did you wash your feet the last time?" and opened the window.

My cellmates chatted a bit and the fat one suffered an attack of self-pity. "Oy, if my sister in Palestine knew that her Yashinka [diminutive of Yasha] has been put here in prison—*for robbery*?!?" After continuing in this vein for a while he suddenly changed his tone. "How much can they give me? Surely no more than 10 years!"

In contrast, the thin one came clean, admitting that he had been caught stealing a car. But he contemplated a career change. "From now on I shall steal only horses. If I cannot sell the horse I shall slaughter it and sell the meat."

My cellmates were picked up the next morning, and a couple of hours later it was my turn. At Police HQ I was led into a large office with a few desks and a steel cage. As soon as my cellmates in the cage spotted me they let out loud cheers, greeting me like a long-lost friend. The policewoman gave me a very suspicious look but after checking my file and hearing my explanation for the warm welcome, she relaxed and whispered to me that Yashinka was not the fittest company, having been charged with armed robbery. Fortunately I was not put in the cage but was ushered into some other room. Before long the door opened and in walked Erica accompanied by **Marille Knauer**, a young

German pharmacist who was then my girlfriend. I had never stayed out all night, so when I had not come home by morning, my mother went to the pharmacy and somehow found Marille whom she had never met. Together they began to look for me. I do not know what other places they tried—surely Marille's knowledge of the city's bureaucracy helped—but apparently they went to the police before visiting the morgue.

I was released but was required to appear in court 2 days later. There was only a single judge, an army major assisted by an interpreter. He surely noticed my black eye and then turned to my assailant. Asked why he carried a blackjack, the boy hesitantly replied that he wanted to protect himself from the many foreigners who lived in his suburb. The next question was why he had attacked me with the blackjack, to which he sheepishly replied, "I do not know". "You'll have 6 months to think about it", the major snapped.

I felt badly about so severe a penalty and later asked the German interpreter whether I could put in a good word for young Mr. Blackjack. He was fairly non-committal, saying I could try to talk to the major but cautioned me that he felt quite strongly about such violence. I never went back and have occasionally regretted it.

WAR CRIMINALS

Federation of Latvian Jews

Soon after the end of the war Jewish survivors began to organize themselves into separate associations by home country, reflecting their cultural and language differences. One was the *Federation of Liberated Latvian Jews in the US Zone of Germany*. We joined it, and Erica became secretary. Some of its members had been liberated by US or British forces and chose not to return to Latvia. Others, especially those who had been liberated by the Red Army, had tried to go back but found that the Soviets were deeply distrustful of any surviving Jews, claiming that Hitler had killed all Jews, so those who survived must be traitors who had collaborated. Some of these survivors never got to Latvia but were detained in camps for collaborators and usually were sent to the Gulag unless they managed to escape. Still others got to

Latvia but changed their minds and sneaked out to the West before the Iron Curtain became impermeable.

One of the latter group was Max Kaufmann from Rīga who had seen his only son murdered by the SS and now was fiercely determined to avenge the crimes of the Nazis and their Latvian accomplices. He became the war crimes representative of the Federation and wrote the (self-published) book *"Churbn Lettland"*—an emotional but not very accurate account of the Holocaust in Latvia. When Kaufmann was preparing to emigrate to the US in early 1948 I was asked in November 1947 to take his place.

My main activity was to find witnesses against war criminals. My counterpart in the *Association of Baltic Jews in Great Britain,* Herman Michelson (no relation to Valerius Michelson), sent me lists of suspected war criminals in British custody, which I forwarded to contact persons in DP camps and in Munich. I then asked anyone volunteering to testify to come to the Federation's office in Munich to prepare a deposition with the help of attorney Jeannot Levenson, the Federation's chairman.

My correspondence with Michelson is preserved in the Wiener Library in Tel Aviv, <http://www.tau.ac.il/Anti-Semitism/wiener.html>. I have copies of most of my letters.

One day I was contacted by Prof. P. Zurkovskis, a Latvian living in a DP camp near Munich, who offered to give me information on Latvian murderers of Jews. When I arrived his wife tactfully left the room, leaving their toddler son behind. The father sprinkled raisins on the bed, saying: "here, son, pick berries", enabling us to talk undisturbed. Zurkovskis, who had been persecuted by the Nazis, was anxious for the murderers to be brought to justice and gave me a list of about a dozen names. I got the list included in a booklet of war criminals published by the Association of Baltic Jews, but I doubt if anything ever came of it. As I recall, the names were from a few small towns in Vidzeme or Zemgale, where all Jews had been killed in July 1941, generally in one day. No Jewish eye-witnesses had survived and there was little chance of locating any of the murderers or Latvian eye-witnesses, let alone getting any of the latter to testify.

The High Command Trial in Nuremberg

Responding to an appeal for witnesses, I went to Nuremberg in July 1948 to testify at the trial of the German High Command. The point at issue was to what extent the German Army had been involved in the extermination of Jews. I did have some pertinent knowledge, because I remembered the letters WM or WH (*Wehrmacht Marine* or *Heer*) on the license plates of military trucks and the insignia of the henchmen involved in street roundups of Jews in Liepāja. My testimony strongly implicated General Field Marshal **Wilhelm Ritter von Leeb**, Commander of Army Group North. The chief of the Evidence Division, Walter H. Rapp, therefore conducted my courtroom interrogation himself. But as the trial had already reached the rebuttal stage, the defense objected a few minutes later on the grounds that it constituted new evidence. After 2 days of legal wrangling, the court sustained the objection, and had my testimony stricken from the record. Too bad, because von Leeb (70)—a vicious anti-Semite since at least WWI—was sentenced to only 3 years.

It was strange to see these famous generals from the topmost ranks of the Third Reich seated in the dock, and even more so, to encounter them in the WC. These wizened old men had been the terror of Europe, but now they stood at the urinals, still in their uniforms but wearing slippers instead of jackboots, each with a towering black MP behind him. Another memorable sight—on the witness stand—was *Gruppenführer* (Major General) Dr. **Otto Ohlendorf**, who had been commander of *Einsatzgruppe D* in Southern Russia. Though already sentenced to death in the *Einsatzgruppen* trial, he was cooperating with the prosecution and now testified about the *Wehrmacht's* role in the killing of Jews. The defense attorney tried to undercut his credibility by concluding the cross examination with the question, "Are you under sentence of death?" Ohlendorf was hanged in Landsberg prison 3 years later. On a visit to the Holocaust Museum I saw a film clip of Ohlendorf's testimony playing continuously on a monitor.

The prosecutor I saw the most of was **Curt Ponger**, a Viennese Jew who had served in the OSS during the war, once parachuting into France in the uniform of an SS major. Ponger

claimed that Ohlendorf was highly intelligent, and wondered
how such an intelligent man could commit such horrible crimes.
I too have often wondered about this question in later years, in
view of the high percentage of university-educated murderers in
the SD.

Some insights come from Ohlendorf's testimony in the
Einsatzgruppen trial, as recounted by prosecutor Benjamin
Ferencz.[35]

> "Another outrageous Ohlendorf argument was that killings by the
> Einsatzgruppen were in self-defense. According to Hitler's
> reasoning, with which Ohlendorf agreed, Germany was threatened
> by Communism. Jews were known to be bearers of Bolshevism,
> and Gypsies could not be trusted. Both groups posed a potential
> threat to the security of the German State. It followed, logically, that
> all such opponents had to be destroyed." Asked about the killing of
> children, "Ohlendorf explained patiently that if the children learned
> that their parents had been killed, they would grow up to become
> enemies of Germany. He was interested in long-range security for
> his country. Hence killing all Jewish men, women, and children was
> a military necessity. Isn't that clear?"

Evidently Ohlendorf, who had joined the Nazi party at age
18, uncritically accepted Hitler's ideology, and although he later
earned degrees in law and economics, he never reconsidered his
early commitment. There is an obvious analogy to religious faith
acquired at an early age.

Indeed, after the death sentence had been pronounced,
Ferencz—impressed by Ohlendorf's intelligence and relative
honesty—asked him whether there was anything he could do for
him (perhaps giving a message to his family). Ohlendorf's bitter
reply was that the Jews in America would suffer for what
[Ferencz] had done. Ferencz was stunned, realizing that *"the man
had learned nothing and regretted nothing"*.

Like Ohlendorf, many Germans had been persuaded by
Hitler's ideology and became his blindly loyal followers. Yet
others, although exposed to the same propaganda and mass
psychosis, rejected part or all of this ideology. One remarkable
example was my boss Paul Schlicht at the construction firm A.
Dehlert, a simple man with only a grade school education.

---

[35] Benjamin Ferencz, http://www.benferencz.org/index.php?id=8&story=33

Though a loyal Nazi party member and an admirer of the *Führer*, he rejected anti-Semitism. He had hired my brother and me despite our second-class status as putative half-Jews and never made any hostile or disparaging remarks. But some months later, Major Bufler, commander of an army construction battalion, told him that these two half-Jews were not to set foot in his unit. Schlicht was quite annoyed, told us that to him a Jewish background made no difference, and sarcastically remarked that the major must be *"ein feiner Mann"* (a fine man). Yet he remained an admirer of Hitler. A few months later, my brother out of boredom made a nicely lettered sign: "What would the Führer say to this?" and put it up on the wall next to our desks. We had seen this slogan in a German magazine, where it was presented as a touchstone for people to judge their actions. But Schlicht, thinking we as half-Jews had meant to brag about our nice, cushy office jobs, angrily told us that he would not allow anyone to make fun of the Führer.

Thus intelligent, highly educated Ohlendorf had uncritically accepted all of Hitler's ideology, clinging to it even when facing the gallows. But simple-minded Schlicht was discerning enough to reject anti-Semitism. Perhaps he had some good experiences with Jews that he chose not to forget. Intelligence and critical thinking do not always go hand-in-hand.

In early 1953, I was shocked to read that my Nuremberg interrogator Ponger and his brother-in-law Otto Verber had been arrested in Vienna, where they had spied for the USSR using their "Central European Literary Agency" as a front. But then I remembered that whenever I said something critical about the Soviets, Ponger always defended them, sometimes contrasting anti-Semitism in the US with its putative lack in the USSR. Ironically, a new wave of anti-Semitism had started in the USSR in 1948, culminating in the 13 Jan 1953 announcement in Pravda of an alleged plot of Jewish doctors against Stalin. But "nobody is as blind as the man who does not want to see".

I spent about a week in the witness house at Nuremberg, sharing a room with 4 other witnesses. Here are a couple of tales by two of them, former Soviet POWs.

One day the starving prisoners received a rare present: a German army horse that had dropped dead. None of them knew anything about butchering, but the two Jews volunteered and were promised the liver as their reward. They managed to carve up the cadaver to everyone's satisfaction and went away to wash up. But when they came back the liver was gone. There was not a scrap of meat left anywhere, except for the horse's penis. Having no other choice they proceeded to boil it. After an hour it still was tough, and it got no better after another 1, 2, 3 hours. Recognizing a lost cause they divided it and started chewing, chewing, chewing. Finally one turned to the other and said in frustration, "A prick we have cooked and a prick we have eaten." (The Russian original takes only 5 words and is punchier).

One of these two prisoners was assigned to work for a German army surgeon, who quickly realized that the prisoner was a Jew—perhaps from his ability to speak some (Yiddish-tinged) German. Knowing that the prisoner would be killed as soon as someone noticed that he was circumcised, he offered to do a surgical restoration that would make it look as if he had been operated on for phimosis. The operation evidently was a success as the prisoner survived the war, but he still remembered the discomfort, telling us in a Yiddish singsong, "So I went around for 3 days with a dick THIS BIG."

Collapse of War Crimes Work

My work on war criminals came to an untimely end in late 1948. Many of the SS men who had been active in Latvia were in British custody, and the prosecutors were preparing a "Rīga Ghetto" trial. They sent requests for witnesses to Herman Michelson in London who passed them on to me. I in turn circulated them among Latvian Jews and arranged for them to file depositions in Munich. But then a number of seemingly distant events caused a collapse of our efforts.

The Western allies had planned a currency reform for all 4 zones of Germany, but when the Soviets continued to balk and obstruct, the Western powers carried out the reform in their 3 zones on 23 Jun 1948. The next day the USSR retaliated by cutting off all rail, road, and water routes to Berlin on the pretext of "repairs" (the water surely needed repairing), so as to starve and strangle West Berlin. Two days later the Allies responded by an airlift that brought all needed supplies, even coal, into Berlin.[36]

After the currency reform it became difficult to bring witnesses to Munich, as both they and the Federation were short of money. Emigration had speeded up, scattering witnesses all over the globe. The Berlin blockade and the intensifying Cold War also made the Allies more dependent on good relations with Germans, causing them to wind down or cancel war crimes trials. The Israel independence war had started on 14 May 1948, and most Jewish organizations refocused their efforts on the new state at the expense of war crime prosecution. The Jewish Central Committee in Munich even sent me an induction notice for the Haganah (precursor of the Israeli Army) and relented only when the Federation urged them to exempt me because of my war crimes work. But the Committee reduced its funding for the Federation and similar organizations, and soon decided to disband them all on 31 Dec 1948. I tried to find a new institutional home for the war crimes effort, but three organizations turned me down.

Things also fell apart for H. Michelson. In early October 1948 the Association of Baltic Jews in Britain voted by a slim majority to stop all work on war crimes, as the chair of the organization, Mrs. Benjamin, and the secretary, Mr. J. Lossos, falsely claimed that the British government would not let them send relief parcels to DPs if they did not cease their war crimes activities. Michelson tried to find other institutional backing and in late October sent me a request from the British Director of Prosecutions for stronger evidence on a number of prospective defendants in the Rīga Ghetto trial. But it had become very difficult to get depositions; prospective witnesses wanted travel expenses and a witness fee, and the Federation—broke for months—was to close on 31 Dec anyhow. I had no choice but to quit. Presumably Michelson did likewise.

---

[36] They built a new airport in 49 days, and at the peak of the airlift, a plane landed every minute. Nearly a year later the Soviets, realizing that they had been licked, reopened the ground routes.

A few months later the British authorities quietly released the suspects in the Rīga Ghetto trial, including the arch-murderer Viktors Arājs (1910–1988), whose commando had killed at least 26,000 Jews in Latvia. As recently as October 1948 the prosecutors had described his case as one of the stronger ones, but unrealistically asked for witnesses who had seen him pull the trigger. After release Arājs lived in Frankfurt under his wife's maiden name until 1975 when he was arrested, tried, and sentenced to life imprisonment. He died in 1988, presumably looking back with satisfaction at the murders and the 26 good years he had enjoyed from 1949 to 1975.

EMIGRATION PROBLEMS

Deeply traumatized by the Holocaust, most Jewish DPs wanted to emigrate to Palestine, the original Jewish homeland from which they were expelled nearly 2,000 years ago. There they hoped to be secure. Jewish return to Palestine had begun in the late 19th century, but the Palestinian Arabs who had been living there for more than 1,000 years soon resented the newcomers. After WWI the League of Nations had assigned (formerly Turkish) Palestine as a mandate to Britain, which then struggled with the ever more difficult task of balancing the conflicting interests of Jews and Arabs. There were Arab riots and uprisings in 1928 and 1936–39, in which they fought against British troops and Jewish police; nearly 6,000 people were killed. Britain severely restricted further Jewish immigration in 1939, but pressures became unbearable after WWII, causing Britain to return the mandate to the UN.

The UN drew up a partition plan in November 1947 that left more than half the country to the Palestinians but gave the rest to the Jews. The Jews accepted the plan but the Arabs did not. Violence grew steadily and after Jews proclaimed the state of Israel on 14 May 1948, troops from 8 Arab countries attacked. Fighting, interrupted by several truces, continued for another year, by the end of which Israelis held 78% of Palestine. Some 700,000 Palestinians had fled or were expelled.

My family had never been Zionist, and Erica and I had no desire to go to Palestine. We felt that the opposing claims of the

Jews and Palestinians would cause perpetual conflict, and we had little in common with the Zionist DPs who were headed for Israel. Instead we wanted to emigrate to an English-speaking country overseas, to get as far from the USSR as possible. England was too close, Canada was accepting only children under 16 or adults willing to work as lumberjacks for 2 years, and Australia also had some strings attached.

The US, looming large after the war, was more appealing. I had learned some tidbits about the US in my geography class 1937–39 (ice water taps in hotel rooms, stores located close to their competitors rather than far away, etc.). In Nazi times we had read propaganda such as a series "God's Own Country?" in the German press but were able to distinguish valid criticism from Nazi exaggerations. A fair amount of the information was truthful, such as the description of 24/7 American drugstores that were so unlike European pharmacies, massive unemployment, the Dust Bowl, multiple license plates on interstate trucks, etc. From 1946 on I read the *New York Herald Tribune* whenever I could and gradually assembled a realistic picture from even minor news items.

One example was the high regard for human life. I recall a huge effort to save a little girl that had fallen into a well; in postwar Europe there might have been just a fatalistic shrug or at best a perfunctory rescue attempt. Even the US Army in wartime had shown such regard, as mentioned in a slightly disapproving tone by the German students in our lab. When encountering resistance from a heavily defended town, US troops did not stage a frontal assault but pulled back and blasted the defenders with a withering artillery barrage. Evidently the US—unlike its enemies and even some allies—viewed artillery shells as much more expendable than the lives of its soldiers.

The US also was more welcoming of immigrants than any other country—a major attraction for me who had been an outsider or foreigner all his life. The balance of power between government and people was much less tilted toward the former than in European countries. Also, I thought that the slogan "Land of unlimited opportunity" was not far from the truth. Soon Erica succeeded in tracking down a first cousin in New

York, Anna Gabrielson Shefts, who was willing to sponsor us. Thus we set our sights on the US.

But my preoccupation with the UNRRA University and some related follies caused a 2½-year delay in our emigration to the US, and nearly kept us out of the country altogether. In April 1946 we had applied for visas to the US and now waited our turn. Under the then prevailing quota system, only 21 people of Latvian birth were admitted each month, worldwide. Prospective emigrants who had passed all formalities thus had to wait in a camp—often for several months—until "quota numbers" became available. I had obtained a scholarship at the University of Oklahoma through the Hillel Foundation and was anxious to leave. I knew that Oklahoma was not a first-rate university like Harvard or Berkeley, but I did not yet know that the quality range of universities in the US was much wider than in Europe. Anyhow, a scholarship was a big attraction to a penniless immigrant.

Edward the SS-Man?

From 1945 to at least 1948 mail in and out of Germany was censored by the Military Government. Somewhere I had seen a notice that prospective emigrants had to have all letters, documents, etc. cleared by the military censor. We had a small suitcase full of papers: my father's ledgers and business correspondence, my brother's letters, etc. In the summer of 1946 I took the suitcase down to the censor's office and yes, they needed to look at everything. When I went to pick up the papers a week later, I was told that they were not ready, as "some Latvian documents have to be translated". Would I please come back the next day at 2 PM sharp?

When I did, a couple of US soldiers were waiting for me and drove me to the HQ of the CIC [Counter-Intelligence Corps], ostensibly to pick up my papers. I was ushered into the building and into an office with the modest sign: *"Into This Room Walk the Sharpest Investigators in Europe"*. The officer behind the desk, flanked by a Pole in civilian clothes, began to quiz me.

CIC: "When were you in Prague and what were you doing there?"
EA: "In September 1945, inquiring at the Swiss embassy about emigration."

CIC: "No, earlier that year, during the war."

EA: "I had never been there before."

CIC: "No that is not true, come clean."

By then I had noticed two sheets of paper on his desk, titled:

> Eduard Alperowitsch, Latvian SS-man, trying to emigrate to US
> Georg Alperowitsch, Latvian SS-man, trying to emigrate to US

Now it dawned upon me what was behind it. My draft deferment carried the stamp of the SS Recruiting Commando Latvia, with the Nazi eagle (Fig. 21). Also, while in Chomutov, I had written a letter to some SS-office in Prague asking for support payments for my mother, as my brother had died from typhoid and diphtheria soon after discharge from the 20th Latvian police battalion, and presumably had contracted these diseases while in service. The SS-office rejected our request, saying that the infection may have occurred after his discharge.[37] Somehow the "sharpest investigator" had missed the fact that my brother had been dead for a year when that letter was written and had not taken the trouble to apply for a posthumous US visa.

> EA: "I was in the hospital for 2 months in early 1945 and bedridden for months afterwards, and have documents to prove it. Tell me exactly when in early 1945—or any other time—I supposedly was in Prague and I will produce an alibi."

But the CIC man refused to get specific and kept going around in circles. Either he or the Pole then had the bright idea of looking for a tattoo of my blood group under my arm. (*Real*, i.e. German, SS-men did have such tattoos, but generally not Latvians or other foreigners in *foreign* SS units. See Ch. 6 and Part II for further details on the differences between German and foreign SS units.)

Having found nothing under my armpits, the Pole suggested looking on the inside of my thighs, claiming that some SS-men had their tattoos there. Again they found nothing. The CIC man had noticed my circumcision, and beginning to waver, he asked the Pole to step behind me so as to be able to communicate with

---

[37] Not likely. Georg was discharged on 14 Dec and got sick some time between 26 and 30 Dec. The incubation period for typhoid is variously given as 10–20 days or 1–2 weeks, but with a range 3–60 days. As he had been living with us since his discharge, all of us would have gotten sick if the infection had happened at home.

eye and hand signals. Perhaps one or both were not sufficiently trained in this skill, because the Pole suddenly spoke up: "For me it is sure!"

I remained very calm throughout and kept asking them to specify the dates of my purported visit to Prague or service in the SS. The CIC man finally gave up and told me where I could pick up my duly censored papers. Our little brown suitcase was sealed with multiple strips of cellophane tape, captioned "OPENED BY MIL. CEN.- CIVIL MAILS". It was another 2 years before we dared open it.

With all due respect for the "Sharpest Investigators in Europe", I wondered why they thought a Latvian Waffen-SS soldier now pretending to be a Jew would submit documents with SS seals and addresses to the censor.

"...Prejudicial to the Interests of the U.S."

Luck seemed to be on our side. In mid-December 1946, only 8 months after our visa application, we were summoned to check into the emigrant camp (*Funk-Kaserne*, a former barracks) in the outskirts of Munich. There we were to wait for several months until we had reached the top of the worldwide queue for the precious 21 Latvian quota numbers. We nominally signed in on 24 December 1946, but actually kept our furnished room in town and visited the camp only briefly each day to see if our names had been posted. But as mentioned above, a major crisis broke out at the UNRRA University in mid-January: UNRRA tried to close it in mid-term, and so we students fought back with sit-ins, hunger strikes, protest marches, etc. On 17 Jan 1947 I was appointed press officer of the student organization and became deeply involved in the struggle. After we had thwarted UNRRA's attempt to dismantle the laboratories, we kept guard day and night.

In the midst of all this excitement, I learned that I was called up on 1 February to a work detail at the emigration camp—the accepted way to make emigrants pay for their room and board. (Students had been exempt until then and again became exempt in March, but it was my tough luck to be there in February). Not having partaken of this room and board, I felt no great obligation to report for work, especially when our university was fighting for its life. Foolishly I therefore went to the camp doctor and asked him to check my fitness for physical labor, because a doctor had predicted in 1945 that I would never fully recover from my myocarditis. The camp doctor examined me and referred me to a commission, which in turn sent me into town for an electrocardiogram. During these proceedings—which took nearly 2 weeks—I was supposed to be excused from work.

Things had gotten very stormy at the UNRRA University, so relying on my medical excuse, I stopped visiting the camp (a 2-hr round trip) and checking the bulletin board. But when I next checked it, I found that I had been summoned to work on 3 consecutive days, though my medical case was still pending. The camp commander, Major C. L. Butler, considered me a malingerer and angrily expelled me from camp without hearing me out or waiting for the doctors' decision. My visa application was suspended and was formally rejected 6 months later by Consul E. Tomlin Bailey, on the grounds that my "admission to the US would be prejudicial to the interests of the country within the meaning of Sec. 58.53 (k)" of the Immigration Act.

As I learned later, Sections 58.53 (a) to (j) deal with enemy agents, subversives, spies, saboteurs, terrorists, revolutionaries, war criminals, threats to public safety or Western Hemisphere defense, etc., whereas (k) includes "any alien...in whose case circumstances of a similar character may be found to exist, which render the alien's admission prejudicial to the interests of the US...". Consul Bailey had gone to the trouble of obtaining a special ruling from the State Department that my case was covered by Sec. 58.53 (k).

I kept writing letters to the consul and to various officials in Germany and the US, and was joined by several Jewish organizations and a few friends or relatives in the US and Canada. All efforts hit a brick wall, and my most sympathetic supporter, Major Abraham Hyman (Assistant to the Adviser on Jewish Affairs at US Army HQ in Frankfurt) finally advised me to get an education in Europe. He added, "Personally, I hope that you may become a renowned scientist and that my country may, in the future, compete for your services".

At last the ice broke in early 1949, when, as I learned, a Mr. H. J. L'Heureux of the State Department expressed interest in "a young DP who had been denied a visa because he had refused to work in a camp".

Presently, in May 1949, we were summoned to the *Funk-Kaserne*, where DPs were now being processed by the thousands under an amendment to the Immigration Act that permitted Eastern European quotas to be "borrowed" from the 21st and 22nd centuries. A kindly man, Vice-Consul McFarland, asked me a few routine questions and then discreetly inquired about my myocarditis.[38] It turned out that the State Department had assumed, on the basis of my 1947 cardiogram, that my claim of myocarditis was a fake. Now that I finally knew what was troubling them, I promptly produced three 1945 cardiograms showing considerable heart damage. They were added to my file, but before granting my visa, Consul McFarland jokingly extracted the promise that I would never become a Communist. Seldom was a promise more willingly given.

We left Munich on 9 June 49 and arrived at a camp in Bremerhaven the next day, where we received our third redundant smallpox vaccination that year—the left hand did not know what the right hand was doing. On about 14 June we boarded our ship, the troop carrier *General Muir*. It was no luxury liner, but we used only the bottom 3 of the 4 tiers of bunks, had bathrooms with showers, no fleas, and ample food. The latter was especially welcome after the Bremerhaven camp, where rations were very skimpy (presumably the larcenous kitchen staff knew that no DP would jeopardize his emigration by complaining at this late stage.) Day after day I consumed 20 slices of fluffy American bread and double servings of most other items, to make up for 8 lean years in Europe.

The sea got a bit rough once we reached the Atlantic, and although I did not get seasick, many other passengers did. They were either too weak or too slow to get to the railing in time, with the result that the decks, stairs, and especially the

[38] I happened to notice on his desk a note from some higher-up, telling him to check whether I was "…OK, that is, not obnoxious," and if so "…to grant a visa on the grounds that his admission is no longer prejudicial to the interests of the US…". Somehow I passed muster.

bathrooms were coated with vomit. Cleaning crews tried their best, but hopscotch became an essential skill.

I volunteered to write for the ship's daily newspaper and turned in a set of tongue-in-cheek stories, such as an appeal for parents to watch their children, as an unattended child had broken the famous Greenwich meridian when we were crossing it, or an announcement of a vomiting contest. The IRO escort officer, a young Frenchman named Robert Weill, greatly enjoyed my efforts but feared that they would be over the heads of many passengers.[39] Nonetheless, he accepted milder versions of many of my pieces.

Weill taught me an interesting lesson. When he asked me what nationality I was I said Jewish, but he gently shook his head and said I was Latvian, though of the Jewish religion. That was my first introduction to the Western definition of nationality, which I now much prefer to the Eastern one.

On 24 June, 1949, we landed in Boston. I remember the smart uniforms of the Massachusetts State Police and the excitement of finally setting foot on American soil. This would be our homeland from now on.

---

[39] UNRRA had metamorphosed into the International Refugee Organization (IRO) in 1947.

10. EPILOGUE: THE REST OF MY LIFE

WORK

AFTER ARRIVING in the US in June 1949, I spent the summer as an inept waiter in a downscale Jewish hotel in the Catskill Mountains, NY, belonging to the husband of my second cousin. I wrote to various universities, only to learn that I was too far along to meet residence requirements for a bachelor's degree. Only Columbia University would take me as an "unclassified" student in their School of General Studies, offering to reconsider my status after my first semester. After receiving two As and two A+s, I found myself in graduate school in early 1950, where I soon was admitted to the Chemistry PhD program. I signed up with J. M. Miller, a brilliant young nuclear chemist only 4 years older than I, who became a close friend and father figure. My high-stakes but fiendishly difficult dissertation topic—search for the "missing" element technetium in nature— eventually turned out to be a wild-goose chase. But when I got my degree in 1954 it still looked cautiously hopeful.

My first academic job, as Instructor at the University of Illinois in Urbana, IL, taught me the huge difference between conservative and liberal universities in the US. More than offsetting this disappointment was the good fortune of meeting my future wife Joan Fleming, nutritionist from Canada. I gladly accepted an offer of an assistant professorship from the University of Chicago, changing my name to Anders when I became a US citizen. A few months later, in November 1955, Joan and I got married. Our children George and Nanci were born in 1957 and 1959.

The University of Chicago, full of people much smarter than I, quickly cured me of the arrogance I had acquired during my education at U. Munich and Columbia. My colleagues were brilliant, inspiring, and generous, treating junior faculty as their equals. As for the institution, I particularly enjoyed an aspect best described by president George Beadle: "I know of no university other than Oxford and Cambridge that has so few rules, which are broken so consistently, as the University of Chicago".

In 1957 I finally got the technetium albatross off my neck, when a new measurement gave a negative result, with an upper limit to the technetium concentration 100 times lower than the positive result I had obtained on the same mineral in 1953. Now I was free to study meteorites, which had been my dream since 1952, when I first saw and touched meteorites. They were extremely ancient—older than the oldest rocks on Earth, and exotic—from distant parts of the solar system unreachable to man. Until the end of WWII they had been studied almost only by classical geologists, but now a number of physicists and chemists had become interested and were using modern techniques and modern ideas to tease out new information. For some years Nobel laureate Harold C. Urey at the University of Chicago was the world leader in this field, aided by a number of brilliant young coworkers. They moved on to other institutions, creating new centers of excellence that revitalized the field. Urey himself went to the University of California San Diego in 1958, so we overlapped only briefly.

My students and I managed to find a few important problems that turned out well and helped me move up the academic ladder, even though I often got embroiled in controversy—particularly with Harold Urey (origin of diamonds in meteorites, claims for extraterrestrial life in meteorites, etc). A sabbatical year at the University of Bern, Switzerland in 1963/64 gave me an opportunity to develop a number of new ideas about meteorites and to combine them into a new model. The resulting review became the most-cited paper on meteorites and continued to influence the field for more than a decade.

After President Kennedy announced a moon landing as a national goal, NASA realized that meteoriticists were some of the best-qualified people for study of lunar samples, as their techniques and ideas were directly applicable to them. Moon rocks thus became a major research topic for my group. We studied samples from all 6 Apollo missions as well as from 3 Soviet missions, and stayed in the lunar sample program until ~1980. But we also continued our meteorite work, earning the usual mixture of praise and attacks.

In the late 1960s, I got into another wild-goose chase: yet another hunt for a new element. Nuclear physicists had predicted that well beyond the known end of the Periodic Table there might be an "island of stability" of superheavy elements, some of which might be sufficiently long-lived to have occurred in the early solar system. They would eventually decay to known stable elements with a characteristic fingerprint. My group and independently two others suggested that a tiny, strange xenon component in primitive meteorites might be this fingerprint. We spent the next 15 years on this quest, occasionally aided by our knack for "doing the right experiment for the wrong reason".

The superheavy element turned out to be a chimera, but in its place we discovered in 1987 a nice consolation prize: *stardust* in meteorites. These are tiny grains of diamond, graphite, and silicon carbide with wildly anomalous *isotopic* ratios, far outside the range of the solar system. Such ratios can form at temperatures above 100 million degrees, as occur in the hot interiors of red giant stars but not even in the center of the sun. It is mind-boggling that we have in hand tiny specks of stardust that formed at distances, temperatures, and times far outside the realm of human experience. Each grain can give detailed information on its parent star: mass, composition, temperature, stage of evolution, etc. By an intellectual tour-de-force nuclear astrophysicists have calculated conditions in various types of stars, but now that we can study stardust with powerful laboratory instruments, we can check these calculations and find new insights. This has become a new, active research field.

In 1985 we stumbled unto another discovery, related to the mass extinction at the end of the Cretaceous period 66 million years ago. Some 2/3 of all known species, including the dinosaurs, became extinct at that time. This long-standing mystery was solved by Alvarez and coworkers in 1980. They found that the thin, dark *boundary clay* layer separating Cretaceous and Tertiary sediments worldwide was more than 1000-fold enriched in the noble metal iridium compared to the sediments above and below. As iridium is very rare on earth but more common in meteorites, they suggested that a giant (~10 km) meteorite had struck Earth at that time. Such an impact, with energy equal to some 100 million hydrogen bombs, would destroy most life on Earth.

Once again we did the right experiment for the wrong reason, dissolving a boundary clay sample in acid. A black carbon residue remained. Under the electron microscope it showed necklace-like chains of tiny beads that are characteristic of soot, proving that the carbon came from a fire. The same kind of soot showed up in 10 other locations from all over the world, so the fire, or at least the smoke, had spread over the globe. The total amount of soot was huge, implying either that all the world's forests had burned down or that coal or oil deposits had also caught fire. A global fire on top of the devastation from the impact would make a bad situation worse: lethal heat, pitch-dark skies, poisoned air, etc.

Over the years I received about a dozen professional honors, including election to the US National Academy of Sciences. My publication list had grown to about 260 papers. I decided to take early retirement at age 65 (in 1991), not only to make room for younger people, but also to "quit while I was ahead". Better that people should ask *Why did he retire* than *Why doesn't he retire?*

FAMILY

Joan and I have had a very happy life, sharing joys, sorrows, and crises in complete harmony. She is wonderfully patient, rational, and levelheaded, providing a happy home for the children and me (Fig. 23).

23. Joan and Edward Anders (2006)

Most of the sorrows and crises in our life, alas, came from my mother. I was her only surviving relative, which greatly aggravated the usual mother-in-law problems. We tried living under the same roof with her for 5 months, but no matter how hard we tried, she was angry, unreasonable, and abusive. At last she attempted suicide, spent a week in a psychiatric ward, and then moved into her own apartment, continuing to see a psychiatrist. (In retrospect it seems very likely that she suffered from schizophrenia.) We continued to see her at least weekly, took her along on trips to Europe, but no matter what we did, there were alternating periods of sunny and stormy weather, occasionally reaching Category 4 hurricane strength. About 3 years before her death in 1992 she got Alzheimer's disease and developed a mellow, cheerful personality. That was a relief for everyone.

George, inspired by his high school journalism teacher, decided to become a journalist. At Stanford he concentrated on economics and journalism. He worked at the Wall Street Journal for 30 years, taking time off to write 3 successful books. During a stint as London Bureau Chief of *The Wall Street Journal Europe* he met his future wife, (American) journalist Elizabeth Corcoran. They married in 1988 and now live in Burlingame, CA with their 2 boys, Matthew and Peter. Soon after Rupert Murdoch bought the *Journal*, George left and has just completed his fourth book. Elizabeth has worked for *Scientific American, Washington Post,* and *Forbes.*

Nanci, having manifested a heart of gold early on, got a master's degree in Social Work at U Wisconsin in Madison and worked in a variety of jobs, from bartending to real estate management. She married David Schiman, now regional sales director at the pharmaceutical company GlaxoSmithKline. They live in Mequon, WI with their 3 daughters: Sara, Amy, and Leah. Nanci is strongly interested in mental health and works at the *Children's and Adolescent Bipolar Foundation.*

After my retirement in 1991 we moved to Bern, Switzerland, where I had often been a visiting professor as guest of Johannes Geiss, Director of the Physics Institute. It took me several years to disengage from science and have time to travel, but then I had a few carefree years before revisiting my past and becoming very busy once again. In 1999 we moved back to the US and settled in Burlingame, CA, near San Francisco.

RENEWING TIES TO LATVIA

I never expected to concern myself in my later years with the Holocaust or with Jewish or Latvian problems in general. But three chance events in 1996/97 got me involved nearly full-time in one such project after another. Each took a lot of time. Most involved controversy and struggle, often with people whose ethical standards were, well, different.

Recovering Victims' Names

I had learned that Yad Vashem in Jerusalem had in 40 years of effort recovered only about 20% of the names of Latvian Jews. Yad Vashem relied on *Pages of Testimony*—"symbolic tombstones"— submitted by survivors, but as only 2% of Latvian Jews had survived the German occupation, it was no wonder that the count was so incomplete.

Soon I found that there exists an excellent source: an unpublished census from late August 1941, the second month of the German occupation. The census records for Liepāja and several other cities are in the Latvian State Historical Archives in Rīga! The organization "Jewish Survivors of Latvia" was not interested in retrieving these records. Instead they sold space at $100/name on a wooden Memorial Board in the Liepāja Jewish Community that could hold 37 names. Evidently the other 6000+ victims were to be forgotten.

With the help of Marģers Vestermanis, director of the Museum *Jews in Latvia* in Rīga, I found a student, Juris Dubrovskis, who copied the names from the census into a laptop computer. He emailed the data to me at the end of his day for review and correction, and thanks to the 8–10 hr time difference, I returned the data to him before he got up the next morning. In addition to the 1941 census, we also used a dozen additional sources in 5 countries, which eventually gave us a nearly complete count of the 7,000+ Jews living in Liepāja on the eve of the Holocaust.

I prepared a memorial book (*Jews in Liepāja/Latvia 1941–45*) and had ~1000 copies printed. They were distributed free: ~800 to survivors or other people with Liepāja roots and ~200 to libraries. The responses were very gratifying. Some people found closure, learning at last what had become of their Liepāja relatives who they thought might have emigrated or fled, or feeling relieved that their names were preserved in libraries and archives. The data also are available on the Web (http://www.liepajajews.org).

Honoring Rescuers

When I learned in 1997 that Yad Vashem in Jerusalem has a special award, *"Righteous Among the Nations"*, for gentiles who

had helped save the lives of Jews, I nominated the two Latvian
ladies (Sofija Zīverts and Herta Kārkliņš) who had falsely sworn
that my mother was German. The awards were granted in 1999.
No descendants of Mrs. Zīverts were found in Latvia, but
descendants of Herta Kārkliņš Burkevics live in Tacoma WA and
accepted the award on her behalf at a ceremony in 2000.

Before the dedication of the Memorial Wall in 2004 I realized
that not a single reminder existed in Liepāja in honor of the
legendary rescuers Roberts and Johanna Seduls. With the City's
permission Vladimir Ban and I therefore installed metal plaques
in Latvian and English on the building where the Seduls couple
had hidden 11 Jews (Fig. 24).

24. *English translation: In this building Roberts and Johanna Seduls hid and
saved 11 Jews in 1943/45. „That's why the name Roberts Seduls/ Will remain
in our memory/ And be inscribed with golden letters/ In Liepāja Jews'
history." (Kalman Linkimer [1912–1987; actually 1913–1988], May 1945.*

Passport Photos

The Latvian State Historical Archives have 11 volumes of
"Passport Issuance Books" from Liepāja, containing passport
pictures. I was deeply moved when I received enlargements of
my grandparents' and other relatives' pictures. Though I still
remembered what they had looked like these pictures vividly
refreshed my memory and, more important, could be shared
with my family. I covered the costs of the pictures for all
survivors for the next 3 months.

Linkimer Diary

The Liepāja janitor Roberts Seduls and his wife Johanna
saved 11 Jews by hiding them in a cellar for 19 months. One of

them, Kalman Linkimer (1913–88), kept an 80,000-word diary in Yiddish, which his heirs tried to sell but without success. Ilana Ivanova—then head of the Jewish Community—pleaded with me to get it translated and published. I explained to her and Linkimer's grand-nephew Igor Skutelsky that there would be *no money in it for anyone*; on the contrary, publishers generally require translation costs and even a publication subsidy for obscure works. Both agreed, and believing them to be honest people, I did not ask for a written agreement. I then spent $14,000 for the translation and some 1,100 hours on editing, but 12 publishers rejected the manuscript. Gunta Gasūna, a young documentary filmmaker operating on a shoestring budget, expressed interest, as did a philanthropist who wanted to print it for free distribution to schools. But Skutelsky and Ivanova thwarted all these projects by demanding large upfront payments, trying to block interviews for the film, and reneging on permission to translate, thus making any publication vulnerable to a lawsuit.

At last, Vestermanis found a way to move forward. Raising funds from the Rīga Jewish Community and a banker who was very prominent in Jewish life, he had the book published by the Museum *Jews in Latvia* for free distribution. Such non-profit publication is exempt from copyright restrictions under Latvian law. Ilana and Skutelsky would hardly risk a lawsuit against three main pillars of the Latvian Jewish Community.

Liepāja Memorial Wall

With Vladimir Ban and two friends in Israel we made plans in 2003 to renovate the Liepāja Jewish Cemetery. Its 4000+ graves had not been vandalized during WWII, but were in disrepair owing to 60+ years of neglect. However, our plans soon were halted by religious objections from the local Jewish Community and by realization of the high costs. We therefore chose a different project: a memorial wall in the cemetery bearing the names of all 6400+ Holocaust and Gulag victims (Fig. 25).

25. *Memorial for 6428 Holocaust and Gulag Victims, Liepāja Jewish Cemetery*

A fundraising appeal to former Liepāja Jews or their descendants brought 164 donations of nearly $24,000. Vladimir Ban organized and supervised construction, and we planned a dedication ceremony for early June 2004. But as a reward for his selfless work several people in Israel poisoned the atmosphere a few months before the event by anonymous false charges, claiming that he had embezzled donations in the 1990s. All my attempts to get these charges investigated by Israeli organizations or officials before the dedication were met by evasions or silence. Only after the dedication was Ban's name resoundingly cleared.

Unfortunately the dedication became a debacle. There were to be 3 secular speakers (President of Latvia, Mayor of Liepāja, and myself) as well as a rabbi and a cantor on the program. Several hundred people, including diplomats from 6 countries, attended. I had asked Ilana to chair the proceedings but she colluded with some Israelis to hijack the ceremony. When my turn came, she called instead on two Israelis: the ambassador and then the vice president of an organization of Latvian Jews. They were accompanied by guerilla theater, involving provocative slogans, waving of a large Israeli flag, and other theatrics. Thus a dignified, low-keyed ceremony honoring Holocaust victims became a strident propaganda platform for the glorification of Israel and defiant challenges to Latvia. My

Ospeech was to outline the WWII crimes as well as the noble deeds of the rescuers. But then I wanted to turn to the present and the future:

> "The damage cannot be undone and the crimes cannot be forgotten. But 3 generations have been born since WWII. So let us work in friendship with them in building a peaceful world. Together, let us try to understand how to prevent dictatorships, wars, and genocide."

Those Latvians who had chosen to come to the dedication surely had friendly feelings toward Jews. But with exquisite finesse, the Israelis greeted them with an "in-your-face" message, as if they were potential murderers: "You will never do that to us again...we are strong now..." underscored by defiantly waving an Israeli flag.

Despite this chicanery, the Wall gave comfort and closure to many survivors, who now knew that the names of their relatives were saved from oblivion and had been placed among the graves of their ancestors. But it has become a major burden for Ban and me, as we searched in vain for a qualified organization to take care of it. Jewish organizations in Liepāja either declined or were disqualified. We completely renovated the Wall in 2008 to ensure a nominal lifetime of at least 50 years and offered to donate it to the City. Our families guaranteed upkeep expenses for 50 years. But at the City Council meeting where the agreement was to be approved, it fell victim to a specious attack by a councilor who happened to be head of the Liepāja Jewish Community. At last we found an idealistic, selfless organization, the Environmental Protection Club of Latvia, that will care for the Wall for 50 years—at no charge.

A Plaque for Non-Jewish Victims

In early 2005, a new charity "Liepāja Jewish Heritage" (=LJH), made plans for a gigantic, 4,000 sq m memorial in Šķēde in the form of a horizontal menorah. We pleaded with them in vain to acknowledge the non-Jewish victims at Šķēde. Some Israelis had independently made the same request, but Ilana Ivanova vetoed it, About a dozen former Liepāja Jews wrote to the mayor about the matter, who then got LJH to agree to install a plaque near the entrance to the menorah, acknowledging the ca. 3,000 Latvian anti-Nazis and Soviet POWs who had been killed at Šķēde along with nearly 4000 Jews.

The giant menorah was dedicated in June 2005 but the place assigned to the "ecumenical" plaque remained empty. Ban and I then asked the City's permission to install a plaque near the mass grave we had discovered in late 2005 (see below), but as the grave is located on the fragile "gray dunes" that are under nature protection, the City offered to us the unused spot on the access path to the menorah. We composed a text in 3 languages, had it approved by the City, and put up a small granite plaque (Fig. 26):

*26. "Ecumenical" Plaque at Šķēde, commemorating **all** Nazi victims (2006)*

MEMORIAL SITE FOR VICTIMS OF NAZI OCCUPATION
Here in the Šķēde dunes were murdered from 1941 to 1945:
3640 Jews, including 1048 children,
~2000 Soviet prisoners of war,
~1000 Latvian civilians,
Including people who helped Jews and prisoners,
and resisted the occupiers.
WE HONOR THE MEMORY OF OUR RELATIVES
AND ALL OTHER VICTIMS WHO LIE HERE,
UNITED IN DEATH.
Donated by Liepāja Jews Edward Anders and Vladimirs Bāns, 2006

This small plaque on the approach path to the giant menorah greatly displeased Ilana Ivanova. Helpfully, a miracle occurred in 2009: 7 young, bushy pines emerged around our plaque, completely hiding it from view. Alas, the City ruled such plantings, whether by heavenly or earthly causes, to be illegal and removed them.

Finding the Mass Graves

I had urged LJH in 2005 to search for the mass graves, and proposed 4 methods at only a small fraction of the cost of the menorah. But they declined, contending that a huge storm in 1957 had eroded about 100–150 m of the coast and washed the graves out to sea.

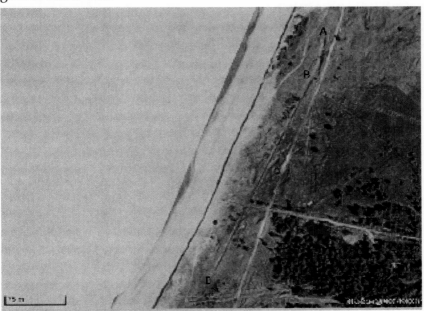

27. *Aerophoto map of Šķēde site. B-E is the largest mass grave*

No evidence of such massive erosion was seen elsewhere near Liepāja and I therefore did the search myself. A high-resolution picture by the US satellite Quickbird indeed showed a ruler-straight, dark line along the coast, right on the military practice range where the executions allegedly took place.[40] The line was about 274 m long, nearly identical to the 265 m ditch

---

[40] War Crimes Trial Against Erhard Grauel and others (Landgericht Hannover, 1968–71).

reported by the Soviet Extraordinary Commission in 1945. The same line also shows up on aerial photos (Fig. 27).

In late 2009 this mass grave became controversial. A consortium "Rapsoil" planned to build 20 wind turbines on the Šķēde dunes, with 1 to 3 towers being very close to the area of the mass graves. The problem could easily be solved by moving these towers inland by 100–200 m, but the firm "Eiroprojekts" that is doing the environmental planning is in deep denial, doubting that anyone was killed at Šķēde, doubting the numbers and ethnicity of the victims, doubting the dates, doubting whether the long ditch is a mass grave, etc. Most of these denials are ludicrous, as there exist mountains of evidence. The last is a serious challenge, however. The Soviets did very limited exhumations, but no records have surfaced except a couple of photos without documentation. At our request, Valdis Segliņš, Professor of Applied Geology at the University of Latvia and his team, have begun a survey with subsurface radar and have found evidence for at least 3 mass graves, near where we and the Extraordinary Commission had suspected them, but spread over a larger area.

Museum "Jews in Latvia"

I am deeply impressed by Marģers Vestermanis, a Holocaust survivor and historian who single-handedly founded and directed this museum and documentation center. For much of its existence it was a shoestring operation with a tiny staff, supported by a few donations and the rental income from Vestermanis' apartment building. It was housed on the top floor of the Jewish Center in Rīga in a few rooms that were last renovated in 1938—maybe in 1939. But Vestermanis has been determined to create a memento of the nearly extinct pre-war Latvian Jewish community. He acquired documents, books, and exhibit items, published excellent scholarly articles, wrote guides to "Jewish Rīga", and compiled a database and 3 TV documentaries on Jews rescued by gentiles and their rescuers. Like a few other individuals I provided some support. A grant from Germany enabled Vestermanis to renovate the ramshackle quarters, and at last his museum gained government accreditation, along with a modest but steady source of support.

He gave me much valuable advice in my projects, and I reciprocated whenever I could.

Occupation Museum

My family and I were impressed by the Occupation Museum in Rīga on our first visit in 1998. I was very glad to find an institution documenting the injustices perpetrated on Latvia from 1940 to 1991: the murders, deportations, exploitations; the suppression of her culture and language; the ruthless colonization. Joan and I went to the Museum on every subsequent visit, and soon got to know its founder, Paulis Lazda as well as a number of staff members. We began to correspond about various matters of mutual interest, and in 2003 I was appointed to the Honorary Board of the Museum. This job does not entail any duties, but I soon became actively involved in the museum's activities, attending meetings of the governing board, reviewing publications and projects, etc. I thoroughly enjoy this work.

RELIGION AND ETHNICITY

My family was only moderately religious, celebrating just 3–6 principal Jewish holidays and attending synagogue on 2 of them. I had Bar Mitzvah at 13 (in 1939) and became fairly observant until the Nazi invasion when my status as a putative half-Jew required me to sever all ties with Judaism. Somewhere along the way I lost my belief that Jews were the Chosen People,[41] which had helped prop up my self-esteem during my childhood. A facile assumption would be that the Holocaust destroyed my belief, but my memory fails to give even the slightest hint that I went that route. Indeed, Jews unable to accept the Holocaust as God's will often completely lose their belief in God, not just in his alleged preference for Jews, but I had merely become an agnostic, not an atheist.[42]

I did learn a lesson from the war and the Holocaust, both of which greatly expanded the range of evil I had thought people

---

[41] The best one-liner on this notion came from Holocaust survivor Marģers Vestermanis in Rīga: „Couldn't He have chosen another people?"

[42] On this question I agree with Carl Sagan's one-liner: "I do not know enough to be an atheist".

capable of. If some Germans and Latvians committed mass murder on a huge scale whereas others remained paragons of virtue then it is absurd to lump together all members of an ethnic group. That conviction has stayed with me the rest of my life, provoking a knee-jerk reaction against any kind of ethnic stereotyping.

After the war I felt no desire to return to Judaism or for that matter any organized religion or ethnic group. I had read some philosophy at ages 17–18 and found a rational approach to ethics more appealing than the faith-based approach of religion.

One seminal experience awaited me on the *"General Muir"*, the troopship that took me to the US in 1949. The IRO (International Refugee Organization) escort officer on the ship, a young, German-speaking Frenchman named Robert Weill, asked me for my nationality, and—accustomed to the system used in Latvia and Germany—I replied, "Jew". No, he explained, he meant my country, and after I said "Latvia" he explained to me the Western concept: I am a Latvian of the Jewish faith. I much preferred this convention though it became less relevant as I Americanized and did not resume ties to Judaism. But east of the Rhine I am still defined by the East European convention, as a Jew first and foremost.

If I am to be defined by membership in a group, I would prefer to be defined on the basis of my closeness to that group: how much do I have in common with any members I might meet by chance? By that criterion I am defined by the following profile, in decreasing order of importance.

1. *Scientist, specifically cosmochemist, or more broadly, physical scientist. This implies a strong commitment to rationality and logical thinking.*
2. *Liberal (in the US sense) with a low tolerance for injustice, but committed to law and order as well as human rights. My attitudes have been influenced by life under Stalin and Hitler and by the Holocaust.*
3. *American, but with a very cosmopolitan outlook and some residual ties to German, Latvian, and Jewish culture (not Jewish religion).*
4. *Lover of classical music of the 18th and 19th centuries.*

5. Not affiliated with any religion but sympathetic to various religions according to their humility and tolerance of heterodoxy.

6. Blood group O positive. Born Jewish.

After drifting away from Jewish religion (and being in almost constant opposition to Israeli policies toward Palestinians), I have asked myself what are the quintessential Jewish qualities that I consider worth preserving and passing on to future generations. I came up with three.

1. Respect for learning
2. Commitment to justice; sympathy for the underdog
3. Jewish humor (nearly always self-deprecating)

My views on religion have changed only slightly over the years. "Reverent agnosticism" still is an appropriate label. My realization of the awesome size, age, and complexity of the universe has not pushed me toward atheism, even though the areas that can be explained by purely inanimate forces keep growing every year. However, I find it hard to believe in an interventionist God who micromanages people's lives, cares about their prayers, professions of faith, diet, attire, and other external observances, and favors followers of one religion over those of another. For all I know, God may not care about anything smaller than a galaxy.

I do accept some of the ethics rules of religion, such as the Golden Rule, Love Thy Neighbor, etc. But I do not believe that these rules, let alone thousands of others, were handed down by God. Even in pre-biblical times each society had some outstanding people smart enough to invent good laws and good ethical rules: the former to be enforced by the state and the latter by the priests. Many philosophers have written thoughtful essays about ethics, using rational arguments rather than threats of divine punishment to promote them. I like my ethics straight, without religious embellishments.

Acknowledgments. I am greatly indebted to my readers: George Anders, Joan Anders, Pēteris Bolšaitis, Anette Campbell, Andrew Ezergailis, Valters Nollendorfs, and Marģers Vestermanis. With impressive unanimity and tact they pointed out weaknesses in the original draft.

Part II. Latvians in WWII: An Evenhanded Analysis

ATVIANS HAVE been widely condemned in East and West for actions during the German occupation (1941–1945). The two main charges are:

1. *Some Latvian paramilitary units killed nearly half of the ~70,000 local Jews as well as some 20,000 German, Austrian, and other Jews deported to Latvia by the Nazis.*

2. *Latvians, many in SS-uniform, fought against the Red Army.*

These charges are true. But neither logic nor fairness justifies the next step many accusers take, blaming *all* Latvians for the crimes of *some*. Crimes are committed by individuals, not by nations. Although collective guilt and collective punishment have been blindly accepted throughout human history, from the Stone Age to the 20th century, at least the democratic countries of the world have repudiated these concepts in 1945 if not earlier. A major reason for this rejection was the ruthless totality of the Holocaust. It denied the humanity and individuality of Jews, demoting them to faceless vermin to be eradicated like rats or bacteria. The defiant post-war slogan, "Never Again" must ban not only genocide but also the first step leading to its justification: collective guilt. To assess the WWII charges against Latvians, we must dig deeper.

I am not the first person to examine these issues, but I do have some credentials that should enable me to offer a fair and accurate picture.

- I experienced the Holocaust in Latvia, losing all but one of my 26 relatives.

- As a putative half-Jew, I was able to live and work within civilian society, able to watch and listen to Latvians and Germans—often unrecognized.
- Being 15 at the start of the German occupation I saw events with a nearly adult eye. My memory—judged elephantine by my scientific peers—has enabled me to retain detailed, accurate recollections of these events.
- My training and life-long work in the physical sciences has taught me to evaluate evidence critically and draw conclusions objectively, considering all relevant, reliable facts but suppressing emotions and prejudices.
- I was actively involved in war crimes investigations in 1947/48, have kept up with Holocaust and WWII history since 1945, and have done research in both areas since 1996.
- I attended Latvian schools, spoke Latvian like a native, and knew hundreds of Latvians, including some close friends.
- I still read Latvian and know many of the important studies by Latvian historians published in recent years.

LATVIAN ANTI-SEMITISM

Some people who have never lived in Latvia, such as Goldhagen,[43] contend that there was long-standing, intense, even murderous anti-Semitism in Latvia. This claim is wide of the mark. Like many other countries, Latvia had a small percentage of vicious anti-Semites, but they never were able to launch a pogrom. Events that triggered pogroms in Russia and some other Eastern European countries never did so in Latvia [Easter, assassination of Alexander II (rumored to be the work of Jews), 1904/5 revolution, Civil War 1918/20, disappearance of a gentile child, etc.] On the contrary, when on 23–24 October 1905 armed Russian ultranationalists ("Black Hundreds") marched on a Jewish quarter in Rīga, Latvian workers helped defend the Jews, and 4 of them were killed.[44] The anti-Semites' predilection for violence had been restrained first by the civilized norms of

---

[43] Daniel Jonah Goldhagen. *Hitler's willing executioners: ordinary Germans and the Holocaust.* New York: Knopf, 1996.

[44] Josifs Šteimanis. *History of Latvian Jews.* Translated from 1995 Latvian and Russian editions; edited and revised by E. Anders. New York: Columbia University Press-East European Monographs, 2002, 38–39 (hereafter cited as Šteimanis).

Latvian society, and after 1918, of the Latvian Republic, where police would not tolerate violent acts against Jews or Jewish property, and the courts were generally fair.

Yes, there was some moderate anti-Semitism in the Latvian Republic (1918–1940). Like the USA and some other countries at the time, Latvia had informal quotas for Jewish university students (except in science and engineering). More so than in the US, Jews were excluded from government positions, but unlike the US, Latvia had no restricted residential communities and few organizations that excluded Jews. Jews were represented in parliament, Jewish schools were state-financed, and Jews owned a large share of trade and manufacturing.

Later the nationalistic dictator Ulmanis (1934–40) nationalized a number of Jewish and German firms to reduce "minority" dominance in some branches of business. But the owners received compensation in hard currency and were free to start new businesses in other branches. For example, after my father's grain mill was nationalized, he leased 5 movie theaters and also resumed my grandfather's grain export business. Ulmanis continued state support for Jewish schools, introduced Jewish religion classes for Jewish pupils in Latvian schools, and banned the anti-Semitic organization *Pērkonkrusts* and its literature. Until its final days Latvia continued to grant visas to Jewish refugees, when most other countries had stopped.[45] All told, Latvia in the 1930's was more anti-Semitic than Italy or Scandinavia; about the same as France, Switzerland, Canada, and the USA; but less so than Germany and several Eastern European countries.[46] People who liken Ulmanis to Hitler and the Latvian Republic to Nazi Germany truly do not know what they are talking about.

---

[45] Karner S., Lesiak P., Strods H. *Oesterreichische Juden in Lettland: Flucht-Asyl-Internierung*. Studienverlag GmbH 2010.

[46] In a novel approach, Anette Campbell has evaluated the extent of Latvian anti-Semitism by analysis of 146 Latvian novels and short stories published 1934–1944. The extent was low 1934–40 and rose to only 4 out of 25 in 1941–44. A. Campbell-Reinsch. *Tradition and Modernity: Images of Jews in Latvian Novels 1934–1944*. (Dissertation, Stockholm University, 2008.)

MURDERERS, ACCOMPLICES, SCOUNDRELS

On 14 June 1941, one week before the German attack, the Soviets had deported 15,443 people, nearly 1% of Latvia's population, to the Gulag or desolate parts of the Far North. Another ~5,000 people were killed or deported before or after this arrest wave, especially prison inmates after the start of war. These persecutions—targeting intellectuals, businessmen, and former government officials, but also farmers, foresters, etc.— caused white-hot anger among much of the population. Jews were nearly 3-fold overrepresented among deportees but few people knew that. Indeed, anti-Semitic feelings increased, because blue-collar Jews, having gained a visible presence in government, Party, and NKVD were viewed as beneficiaries and supporters of the regime. The deputy chief of the NKVD was an Ukrainian Jew, Semyon Shustin, causing many people to assume that the whole organization was dominated by Jews.[47]

Despite this anger, there is no credible evidence—except for a few murders in Rīga—for spontaneous killings of Jews in the interregnum (hours to days) between the retreat of the Red Army and arrival of the Wehrmacht, or in the earliest stages of the German occupation. The Latvian-Jewish historian Marģers Vestermanis has investigated every such claim, but concluded: *"It was an ideal opportunity to settle accounts with Jews, a unique chance for pogroms and massacres. But nothing happened. Nowhere!"* In the only confirmed murder case the motive was robbery, not anti-Semitism.[48] Murders were started not by individual civilians but by German Einsatzgruppe A teams (*Einsatzkommandos*, abbreviated EK), sometimes with help from the Wehrmacht.

---

[47] That had been true in the past. From 1934 to 1936 Jews had filled 39% of NKVD leadership positions in the USSR, but by mid-1939 their share had fallen to 3.5% because of purges. [N.V. Petrov, K.V. Skorkin, et al., eds., *Kto rukovodil NKVD, 1934–1941: Spravochnik* (Moscow: Zven'ia, 1999), p. 495)]. Recent studies show that the number of Jewish NKVD men in Latvia was small; in the Peoples Commissariat of State Security (VDTK) only about 25 of 200 officials were Jews; Aivars Stranga, *Ne pēc nacionālās piederības (Not according to ethnicity)*, Latvijas Avīze, 8 April 2008. A. Stranga. *Ebreji un diktatūras Baltijā. 1926–1940* (Jews and Dictatorships in the Baltics), 2nd edition, Rīga: SIA N.I.M.S., 2002, pp. 516–26.
[48] M. Vestermanis "Es geht um das Warum und das Wie." *Die Tageszeitung* (Berlin), *22.6.1991*, and personal communication.

They were soon joined by handpicked Latvian murder squads, at first in civilian garb to pretend popular rage, then in uniform.

Murderers and Accomplices

Ezergailis (l. cit.) gives an extensive account of the Latvian units involved in the Holocaust. It has been confirmed and supplemented by later studies.

One major task of Einsatzgruppe A was to organize a volunteer "Self-Defense" or "Auxiliary Police" force to replace the Soviet "People's Militia". Under German command, they were to round up Red Army stragglers and communists and assume police functions. A second task in the larger cities, handled more discreetly, was to organize murder units that were willing to "cleanse" the country, i.e. execute "enemies" as defined by the Einsatzgruppe, including Jews. For these murder units the Einsatzgruppen tried to seek out people whose relatives had been murdered or deported. Their anger could be redirected against Jews by the massive, vicious anti-Semitic propaganda that had flooded the Baltics since 22 June 1941.

In Rīga, the Auxiliary Police force was organized on the very first day of the occupation, 1 July 1941. The murder unit—the Arājs Commando, organized as a Latvian SD unit by Viktors Arājs—began to form on the second day. It comprised more than ~100 men by the end of July and peaked at ~300 in November. Despite its limited strength the Commando in July and August 1941 engaged in a murder spree in both Rīga and the provinces. Part of the unit stayed in Rīga, killing about 5,000 Jews and communists in the Biķernieki forest, while a roving team traveled in the notorious "blue buses" to more than a dozen small towns, killing all Jews. The local Latvian auxiliary police usually arrested and guarded the Jews and organized the digging of pits, but in some towns they also took part in the killing.

By mid-December more than 90% of the Jews in Latvia had been killed, and although the Arājs Commando eventually grew to about 1,200 men, most of them were deployed outside Latvia, conducting executions and brutal anti-partisan activities. The Commando killed at least 26,000 people (including 22,000 Jews) in Latvia and some 30,000 in Minsk and elsewhere. Several other murder units briefly existed in Jelgava, Ilūkste, Valmiera, and other cities for the purpose of killing local Jews.

From 1944 to 1967, the USSR conducted criminal trials against 356 captured members of the Arājs Commando. (Many others had fallen in combat but a substantial number, having surrendered to the Western Allies in the last weeks of the war, escaped prosecution.) The Latvian historian Rudīte Vīksne has carefully analyzed the NKVD trial records according to age, education, year of and reasons for enlistment, penalties, etc.[49] The most common penalty was 25 years of hard labor, but ~12% were sentenced to death. Her paper is a unique source of information on the background and mentality of these men.

The original Nazi plan had been to incite the local population to carry out pogroms and mass killings immediately after arrival of the Germans. They were to be filmed and photographed to prove that these were spontaneous "self-cleansing" actions by local people. Although these efforts succeeded in Lithuania, they largely failed in Latvia, as the Einsatzgruppe A report complained:

> "It was significantly more difficult to start similar cleanup operations and pogroms in Latvia. However, after exerting appropriate influence on the Latvian Auxiliary Police, it was possible to initiate a Jewish pogrom in Rīga [on 4 July 41] during which all synagogues were destroyed and approximately 400 Jews were killed". (Quarterly Report of *Einsatzgruppe* A, 15 Oct 41).

Actually this „pogrom" was carried out not by the Latvian Auxiliary Police but by the Arājs Commando in civilian clothes, to imply spontaneous „self-cleansing" by the people.

The people of Daugavpils also were reluctant to engage in „self-cleansing":

> "The Latvians, including the leading active ones, have so far behaved passively toward the Jews, and did not dare rise against them... as opposed to the active attitude of the Lithuanians, the

---

[49] Rudīte Vīksne, „Members of the Arājs Commando in Soviet Court Files: Social Position, Education, Reasons for Volunteering, Penalty." In *The Hidden and Forbidden History of Latvia Under Soviet and Nazi Occupations 1940–1991*, ed. Valters Nollendorfs, Erwin Oberländer, 188–206. Rīga: Institute of the History of Latvia, 2005, hereafter cited as Vīksne, *Arājs Commando.*

Latvians have hesitated to organize and mobilize themselves against the Jews."[50]

Except for Rīga and Jelgava, where the Latvian Arājs and Vagulāns Commandos began to kill Jews in the first few days of the occupation, the killing in other cities was initially done by German *Einsatzkommandos* (EK): more than 400 Jews by EK2 in Liepāja and 1,150 by EK1b in Daugavpils. Several weeks or months later, Latvians began to take over, but Germans generally ordered the executions and were discreetly present at nearly all of them.[51]

Indeed, even with the increasing involvement of Latvians, more than half the murders were carried out by Germans. The largest mass murder, at Rumbula near Rīga (25,000 Jews on 30 Nov and 8 Dec 1941), was carried out by only 36 German marksmen in 3 shifts, all from the personal staff of SS-General Jeckeln.[52] About 1,700 accomplices (including ~1,500 Latvians of whom ~800 were Rīga precinct police) assisted by clearing the ghetto, escorting the Jews on the 10 km march to Rumbula, forming the gantlet to the pit, and guarding the periphery.[53] Some 600–1000 Jews were killed during this "clearing", but the use of automatic weapons and the known brutality of the SD and guards suggests that they rather than the precinct police were the principal killers. In Daugavpils, a unit of EK3 killed 9,012 Jews and 573 communists in July and August 1941. German SD also contributed one of the 3 firing squads that killed 2,749 Liepāja Jews in December 1941. Large contingents of auxiliary police became accomplices in these massacres by arresting, guarding, and escorting Jews. (Ezergailis estimates ~1000 in addition to those in Rīga, but a rough calculation based on actual execution numbers suggests ~2000.)

---

[50] Ereignismeldung Nr. 24, 16 July 1941.

[51] SD Chief Heydrich had directed the Einsatzgruppen to support local efforts of "self-cleansing" but ensuring that this support cannot be traced back to Germans. Indeed, execution pictures taken by the SS never show Germans, but many of those taken by the Wehrmacht do.

[52] The names of 7 executioners and a wealth of other hard-to-find details are given in Anita Kugler, *Scherwitz, Der jüdische SS-Offizier*, Köln: Kiepenheuer & Witsch, 2004, 193–223.

[53] Ezergailis, *Holocaust*, p. 21.

In many murder units, the killing was done by volunteer teams who either enjoyed it or at least could be motivated by incentives such as a few bottles of vodka—a valuable currency on the black market. This division of labor enabled others, such as drivers, interpreters, radio operators, etc. to avoid "getting blood on their hands". But Friedrich Jeckeln (Higher SS- and Police Chief Ostland; hanged in Rīga 3 Feb 1946), who used 36 members of his personal staff for the Rumbula murders, wanted the remaining staff to share the guilt, ordering them at least to watch the executions. In some German units, the commander permitted men to opt out of executions, but peer pressure kept such defections to a minimum.

Rapists

Some rapes were committed in small towns where Jews were arrested one or more days before execution. The few guards, not being supervised during the night, occasionally colluded to seize a young girl and gang rape her. That was less likely to happen in larger cities where Jews often were arrested and shot the same day, and where many guards and supervisors were involved. But opportunities for rape also existed when police entered Jewish apartments, as during the clearing of the Rīga ghetto for Rumbula. Indeed, there is a credible report by survivor Ella Medalye that 8 of a dozen young Jewish women were taken, one by one, from the basement of the Arājs Commando building in Rīga to an upper floor orgy where they were raped.[54] She herself was spared when a compassionate young member of the Commando hid her.

Tormentors

Jews often were beaten, humiliated, or otherwise abused in prisons and at execution sites, by both German and Latvian murder units. Linkimer recounts a number of particularly barbaric atrocities by the German SD in Liepāja, some of them in a public square.[55] Other accounts report savage beatings when Jews in Liepāja and Jelgava were driven through a gantlet of

---

[54] David Silberman. *The Latvian Jewish Courier* **23** [3], 3–6 (2005)
[55] Linkimer, 5–6.

German soldiers to the execution pit.[56,57] Beatings on the street seem to have been rare, although a German newsreel from July 1941 shows a civilian beating a Jew in Rīga. Verbal abuses were more common at least in the early days of the German occupation.

Ghetto and camp guards are also included in this category. Some few were humane but most were brutal, even sadistic, to various degrees. In survivor accounts German guards and German "kapos" often are accused of particularly egregious brutality, but that may reflect mainly their greater numbers and greater power. Latvian guards and Jewish kapos were no altar boys. Some survivors claim that German and Latvian guards were somewhat more lenient toward Jews from their own countries.

Looters

Extensive looting ("night actions") took place in Rīga in the summer and fall of 1941. Small groups of Latvians entered Jewish apartments demanding valuables and grabbing anything else they wanted. Sometimes they even took away men who then were never seen again. Many of these looters were auxiliary police or Arājs men, and some of them were arrested by less larcenous police. But common criminals soon joined the racket.

In some smaller towns the belongings of murdered Jews were distributed to "deserving" people. But by late fall, when large mass executions took place in the cities, the process was well organized to ensure that all belongings of the victims were collected, mostly for shipment to the Reich. Apartments of the victims were sealed so the contents could be removed later. All such Jewish belongings became property of the Reich. Himmler himself had ordered that looting was to be punished by death:

"...these riches shall, of course, be diverted to the Reich without exception. ...[according to my order] he who takes even one mark

---

[56] Ernst Klee, Willi Dressen, Volker Riess. *The Good Old Days: The Holocaust as Seen by Its Perpetrators and Bystanders*. New York: Konecky & Konecky (1991), 126–134.

[57] Wolfgang Leydhecker, *Eine Jugend im Dritten Reich: Nicht wie die anderen*. Darmstadt: Eduard Roether, (1992), 89–91.

of it, that's his death. A number of SS-men—not very many—have violated that order, and that will be their death, without mercy."[58]

In practice, punishment often was less severe. Some Latvian auxiliary policemen who arrested Jews filled their pockets with "souvenirs", and some Latvian civilians and German Navy sailors in Liepāja were caught by the police breaking into Jewish apartments sealed after the December 1941 massacre. German SD men physically fought each other over Jewish belongings left in the Liepāja ghetto after the inhabitants had been transported to Rīga in October 1943, undeterred by Himmler's order or the fact that their boss Kügler was serving an 8-month prison term for stealing Jewish property.[59]

Informers

One class of scoundrels did not lift a hand against Jews or even say an unkind word to their face, but had no qualms about delivering them to their death by reporting them to the police. Hiding with a gentile or seeking to escape into the forests or to Sweden were particularly grave offenses (all aggravated by the concomitant evasion of forced labor), but there were many others: getting food (by barter or by charity), failing to surrender proscribed items such as valuables, radios, or cameras, walking on the sidewalk rather than in the gutter, failing to wear the yellow star, etc.

It is not easy to understand the motivation of these informers. Material gain was at best a minor consideration, as any bounty paid was modest, and the belongings of the victim were supposed to go to the state rather than to the informer. A likely explanation is intense but cowardly anti-Semitism. The informer was so eager to destroy a Jew that he was willing to send a fellow Latvian to prison, concentration camp, or even death. Fortunately the informers were often thwarted by decent people, as we shall see later.

---

[58] Heinrich Himmler. Speech at Posen, 4 Oct 1943. Translation of Document 1919-PS, International Military Tribunal, Nuremberg.

[59] Linkimer, p. 32.

RESCUERS, HELPERS, AND OTHERS

The historian Marģers Vestermanis has spent decades collecting information on Latvian rescuers and in 1998 published a definitive account of this topic.[60] Most of the information in this section comes from Vestermanis, including his latest updates of the numerical data.[61] The known number of Jews hidden by Latvians has risen to 472 (not all survived), and the number of rescuers to at least 400–450, assisted by ~1100 family members. Still more Jews would have been saved, had 37 of the rescuers not been arrested with the Jews they had hidden; at least 27 of them paid with their lives for their good deeds. To hide a Jew took far more courage in Latvia than in Denmark or Holland, as the penalty was death or a deadly concentration camp rather than a reprimand or a brief prison term.

For a better appreciation of the rescuers, one must consider the risks and burdens involved in sheltering Jews. Even those who eluded the police had the huge task of feeding the fugitives for up to 3 years. The rescuer's food ration of 1,200–1,500 calories/day was too little even for herself, and so she had to get additional supplies from the black market or from farmers. Most Jews by then had been robbed of their belongings and could contribute no money or valuables for their upkeep. Especially in cities (where most people lived in small apartments) it was hard to conceal from neighbors the large amounts of food going in and other signs of an increased number of people: voices, footsteps, toilet flushes, laundry, etc. Marion van Binsbergen Pritchard, who participated in rescues of 150 Jews in the Netherlands, once was asked by the local grocer whether she was hiding any people in her house. Why? "You are buying so much toilet paper."

---

[60] Marģers Vestermanis. „Retter im Land der Handlanger. Zur Geschichte der Hilfe für Juden in Lettland während der 'Endlösung'". In *Solidarität und Hilfe für Juden während der NS-Zeit. Vol. 2. Regionalstudien Ukraine, Frankreich, Böhmen und Mähren, Österreich, Lettland, Litauen, Estland.* eds. Wolfgang Benz, Juliane Wetzel. (Metropol: Berlin 1996, 231–271; hereafter cited as Vestermanis, Retter).

[61] Marģers Vestermanis. "Opposition to the Holocaust in Latvia", in *Latvia's Jewish Community: History, Tragedy, Revival,* ed. by Leo Dribins, Armands Gūtmanis, and Marģers Vestermanis (Rīga: Ministry of Foreign Affairs of the Republic of Latvia, 2004). http://www.mfa.gov.lv/en/ministry/4265/4299/ and personal communication, 2010.

Some Examples of Rescues — Successful or Failed

For a nuanced view of Latvian attitudes and actions during the German occupation, it is helpful to review some specific examples.

The most famous rescuer was the Rīga dockworker **Žanis Lipke**, who with his wife, son, and 29 helpers saved 56 Jews. He tried to buy a large fishing boat in order to take a group of Jews to Sweden but was arrested. Released through a bribe, he hid Jews in his house and in the cellars of 6 apartment buildings in the center of Rīga. Then he bought a farm house in Dobele (72 km from Rīga) where he built a well camouflaged bunker. His truckdriver friends gradually took 28 Jews to Dobele, hiding them under hay or firewood. As the bunker was filling up, Lipke recruited the parish elder and the chief doctor of the local hospital, who helped him find several neighboring farms to shelter the overflow. Not all of those Jews survived. Some of them left their refuge in Dobele too soon and were caught.[62]

Another outstanding rescuer was the former sailor **Roberts Seduls** in Liepāja, who as janitor built a hiding place in the basement of a building in the center of town. Designed for 4 Jews, it eventually held 11, who survived there for 19 months to the end of the war.[63, 64] He and his wife **Johanna** provided them with food, a radio, and 6 handguns. Although some neighbors, seeing a big pot on the stove or noticing the large amounts of food he bought every day, suspected him of sheltering fugitives, they never reported him to the police. Tragically, Seduls was killed by a Soviet shell 2 months before the end of the war.

Some of Seduls' „wards" got help from Latvians before finding shelter in the hiding place. **Riva Zivcun** and her 4-year-old daughter **Ada** were led out of the Rīga ghetto by a Latvian policeman **Avots**, who nonchalantly reported to the guard: „Corporal Avots, with wife and child". She first stayed with Avots' girl friend but had to leave when it turned out that Ada

---

[62] Šteimanis, p. 139.

[63] Linkimer, 26–154.

[64] Rebecca Margolis and Edward Anders. "The Linkimer Diary: How 11 Jews Survived the Holocaust". In: *Problems of the Holocaust Research in Latvia*. Rīga: Symposium of the Commission of the Historians of Latvia, v. 23, 2008, 48–71; hereafter cited as *Symposium*.

spoke only Yiddish. Avots then helped Riva find a pre-war acquaintance with whom she stayed for a few weeks. She then returned to Liepāja—now officially „judenfrei"—where she was warmly welcomed in the middle of the night by a female janitor. The Latvian doctor Zandbergs whom she had known before the war gave her medical care without batting an eye, and a Latvian woman, Otilija Šimelpfenigs, agreed to keep little Ada—too young for the hiding place—until the end of the war. Although Ada didn't speak a word of Latvian, Otilija somehow managed to persuade everybody that she was a relative from the countryside.

Several other Latvians sheltered sizeable groups (6–8) Jews: the Latvian marathon champion **Artūrs Motmillers, Voldemārs Didrihsons, Andrejs Graubiņš, _Kauķītis, Alma Pole, Elvīra Rone, Bernets Rozenbergs, Edgars Zande, Arsenijs Korņilovs, Vladimirs Vuškāns, Frīdrihs Rozentāls**, and others. Each of them took on the huge burden of feeding and hiding 6 or more people, knowing that the slightest misstep could mean death for them all.

Some new facets come from the story of two 16-year-old boys in Liepāja, **Israel Alīte** and **Abram Fleischmann**.[65] During the intense manhunt for men over 16 on 22–25 July 1941, both boys were arrested by a Latvian policeman who took them to the Women's Prison, the last stop before execution. There the Nazi-appointed warden **Fricis Klāsons** kept the boys waiting while sending men off in trucks for execution. Curfew for Jews had begun by the time the last truck had left, so Klāsons had the boys fed and put in a cell for the night with 4 or 5 other boys, promising to release them all in the morning. He kept his promise, pretending that they were only 14 or 15 years old.[66]

---

[65] I. Alīte, Interview by B. Černobrova, 28 May 1993. File III/923, Museum „Jews in Latvia", Rīga.

[66] It is not clear how Klāsons, owner of an ice cream parlor before the war and lacking any background in law enforcement, became prison warden under the Nazis. Although he continued to follow orders to send adult Jews to execution, he repeatedly saved young boys, first by misrepresenting their age and later, when even women and children were being killed, by personal intervention. I know of one survivor, then 13 years old and a friend of his son, whom Klāsons spotted in the prison and released. Klāsons seems to have had misgivings about the job and quit soon after the December massacre. He then worked at the same company where I did, occasionally saying a few friendly words in Yiddish. But I never asked him why he quit his prison job.

During the mass arrests for the 15–17 December 1941 massacre both boys again were taken to the Women's Prison, but sneaked out with the workers of Navy Inspector **Friedrich Kroll** and several craftsmen who were released. Caught again but claiming to be the craftsmen Itkin and Schefkin whose names they remembered, they were taken to the Women's Prison for confirmation, where the deputy warden Jurašs asked for their addresses. Israel was able to give the correct address but Abram gave a wrong one. When they begged the Latvian woman who kept the roster to let them out she replied, „If it were up to me I would let *everybody* out". Then she whispered something to Jurašs who relented.

All these months the janitor Mrs. **Indriksone** with her husband and son had helped them, providing food and information and arranging for them to spend nights with their acquaintances, the **Embrekts** family. For the next 6 months, until the ghetto was established on 1 Jul 1942, they stayed with friends of Mrs. Indriksone: **Janaite**, **Kandēvica**, **Ivanova**, **Ģinters**, and also in 3 empty or still occupied Jewish apartments.

Later they stayed with Mrs. **Margrieta Eniņa** and her son **Kārlis** and alternately with their 18-year-old Latvian friend **Jānis Sproģis**. All survived the war.

Not all attempted rescues had a happy ending. I told in Ch. 5 how my father **Adolf Alperowitz** while hiding in our apartment was twice reported to the police by janitor **Hippe**, and was then found, arrested, and shot in December 1941.

Another rescue was similarly foiled by an informant. **Scheine-Rachel Jakobi** (44) and her daughter **Yente** (17) were hidden by **Elizabete Dombrovska**, then by **Olga** and **Jānis Rāts** (late 1944 till the beginning of 1945), and finally by the **Zolman** family. According to the account of her daughter Erika who survived the war in the USSR, in early 1945 Mrs. Jakobi, apparently breaking under the strain of more than 40 months in hiding, suddenly got the idea that her husband—though shot on the street on 29 6 1941 on his way to a doctor—was looking for her, and rushed out to her old apartment. A neighbor reported her to the police. Another neighbor then saw mother and daughter being taken to Šķēde.

A rescue attempt that ended with the death of 4 Jews and 6 rescuers occurred in Aizpute, a small town 42 km from Liepāja.[67] **Žanis Pūķis** (1910–1944), a clerk in the police office, in September 1943 overheard a remark that the Jews working in the local peat factory will be "sent away". His brother **Kārlis** (1919–1944), a tailor in the factory, then warned two Jews who worked for him. Both Pūķis brothers, helped by neighbor **Gerhards Šusters** (1914–1944), then quickly set up a temporary hiding place in the attic of the old Aizpute castle where several Latvian families lived, including **Ieva Dzene** (1892–1944), the mother of both brothers' wives. As arranged, the two Jews then came to the castle that evening, bringing along two other Jews.[68] All moved into the hiding place. In the next few days the three men then dug a bunker behind the Šusters house with 4 sleeping places, a camouflaged entrance, and an emergency exit.

The Jews moved into the bunker and did sewing jobs for farmers, who paid Kārlis in food. But the food did not suffice, and the factory director **V. Kobilko** (who knew that the Jews had gone into hiding but had merely told the police that they had „escaped") suggested that the Pūķis brothers take some potatoes belonging to the factory that were stored in the castle cellar. But someone living in the castle had noticed the removal of the potatoes and reported it to the police. The police searched the castle, and spotting electric wires leading to the attic, found the temporary hiding place. Apparently tipped off by the informer the police went to the Šusters house and arrested Gerhards as well as his father **Jānis** (1880–1944). They did not find the bunker, though. Next they arrested the Pūķis brothers, their wives **Elza** (b. 1920) and **Anna** (b. 1916), and their mother-in-law Ieva Dzene.

After the police had left, the 4 Jews fled to the peat bog, taking along a sawed-off military rifle that Anna had given them. She had obtained it from a deserter from the Latvian Legion

---

[67] Šteinbergs, Ilmārs. Letter to M. Vestermanis, 28 Oct 1989. File III/785, Museum „Jews in Latvia", Rīga.

[68] Yossel Getz (1913–1943), Isaac Heifetz (1909–1943), Shlomo Uzdin (1912–1943), and Leib Uzdin (1914–1943). The Uzdin brothers were from Lithuania, the others from Rīga. Their occupations were: physician, teacher, tailor, and merchant.

named Krūmiņš whom Anna was hiding. A day or two later the Jews killed themselves in the bog. Probably they heard shots nearby and thought the police had tracked them down. Actually the policemen were merely hunting.

The rescuers were taken to a Liepāja prison. Anna, being pregnant, was released after some time. Gerhards was kept in prison about 9 months and then shot at Šķēde with several others. The remaining 5 prisoners were taken to Stutthof with a prisoner transport on 10 October 1944. Ieva died in the arms of her daughter Elza on Christmas night, 1944. Jānis Šusters and the Pūķis brothers did not return from Stutthof and presumably perished in December or January, when the mortality had become very high.

Only Elza survived. In February 1945 she started on a death march. Anybody who fell down was shot. She was liberated by the Red Army in March. Only 3 prisoners were still alive; 11 others had died the previous night. After 3 months in the hospital she returned to Aizpute, her health permanently damaged.

Historian Šteinbergs asked Elza Pūķe whether she understood the risk of sheltering fugitive Jews. She replied: „We understood this quite well, but these people needed to be saved".

LATVIAN ATTITUDES TOWARD JEWS, 1941–45

This question was not studied during the Second Soviet Occupation, as the regime denied a specifically Jewish Holocaust, accused survivors of spying for the Nazis, and accused rescuers of sheltering Jews only for money. Nonetheless, 5 decades later Vestermanis was able to reconstruct an authoritative picture from a very large number of sources: interviews or memoirs of survivors and rescuers, Latvian newspapers, and German documents. I have again drawn heavily from his account.[69]

Vestermanis points out that the traditionally good Latvian-Jewish relations became strained by the growing nationalism of the Ulmanis regime (1934–40), which began to reduce Jewish

---

[69] Vestermanis, *Retter.*

dominance in business under the slogan "Latvia for Latvians". They deteriorated further during the first Soviet occupation (1940/41). Upper-class Jews and Latvians were both persecuted as class enemies, but whereas many Latvians deeply resented the loss of Latvia's independence and for the first time in their history began to look to Germany for help, many Jews felt less of a stake in independent Latvia. Fearing Hitler, many Jews, especially of middle and lower classes, tended to view the USSR as the lesser evil or even a protector.

Soviet deportations and terror had enraged society to a high degree, making not a few people more receptive to massive Nazi propaganda that blamed Jews for all Soviet crimes, as well as fictitious crimes such as ritual murder of gentile children, conspiracy for world domination, and intent to exterminate the Latvian nation. Another factor was the German conquest of Europe in 1940/41, now followed by a seemingly unstoppable thrust into the USSR with capture of millions of POWs. Even though many people rejected Nazi propaganda and were shocked by the mass murder of Jews, they realized that opposition was futile and might jeopardize Latvian prospects in the post-war *"Neuordnung Europas"* (New European order).

Within a few months the mood changed. The Nazis showed no intent to restore Latvian independence, banning displays of the national flag and appointing a pale shadow of a puppet government, called "self-administration" rather than government and composed of "directors general" rather than ministers. Virtually all powers remained in the hands of Germans. Murders of Jews, initially limited to men at least in the cities, now extended to women and children. The German advance slowed down, stalled, and then was turned back at Moscow in December 1941. And the US entered the war.

Campaign Against "Jew-Pitiers"

From Day 2 of the occupation the Latvian press was run by handpicked journalists loyal to the occupiers, dutifully printing Nazi propaganda and announcements.[70]

"The Latvian people never again will have a common homeland with this disgusting race...all pity is in vain, the Jews as a people must

---

[70] I have again drawn heavily from Vestermanis *Retter*.

die. ...Latvians who with their names and deeds are trying to help Jews, and wrongly without reason try to show compassion to Jews—these henchmen of the Latvian people...In the fight against the Jewish inquisitors there must be no pity in our hearts...Now there is no room in the world for Jews...whining and pity are out of place...Woe unto those who want to interfere with our completion of this task...Woe unto those who stand in our way..."

But again and again the papers sounded an exasperated note:

"Some Latvians are still friendly toward Jews...are traitors to their nation by showing compassion...have cowardly soft hearts...have a criminally flexible conscience...have the bad habit of greeting Jews. Any compassion is a crime; if a Latvian really cannot manage without Jews, the gates of the internment camp of his "friends" are open to him, etc. etc."

The Rīga paper „Tēvija" had 5 such articles with massive threats in July 1941 alone. The Smiltene paper „Tālavietis" had 3 broadsides in 3 weeks in July-August 1941, including a threat to "publish the names of all «Jew friends and pitiers» who still talk to Jews, help them, and express their compassion." The Ventspils paper „Ventas Balss" had 5 such reprimands in July 1941, the Daugavpils paper „Daugavas Vēstnesis" had 4 in October 1941, and papers in Jelgava, Talsi, and many other towns delivered similar, repeated blasts.

The editors were frustrated that many of their fellow Latvians evidently were ignoring these cannonades and threats. Had there been only a few "Jew lovers" the editors might have ignored them and let the police deal with them. But these repeated attacks suggest that many people were involved— people who had known Jews for decades and knew that they were not demons, henchmen, or murderers. That was a serious problem for the Nazis and their collaborators. If the Nazi postulate that Jews are the source of all evil in this world is rejected, then Jews are fellow humans with all their virtues and vices, and killing them is murder. Two pastors whose sermons condemned the killing of communists and Jews got off lightly, with a warning by the Security Police. But a deacon who gave an advent sermon on the topic "Thou shalt not kill" was imprisoned and eventually perished in Stutthof.

Even the German Security Police complained that events in Latvia did not follow their expected "self-cleansing" scenario of enraged natives attacking Jews with pitchforks and crowbars. Although Latvian murder teams in Rīga, Jelgava, and a few other cities willingly served as executioners, the hand-picked police chiefs and mayors were curiously hesitant at first. Only at the end of July was the SD able to report "self-cleansing efforts in Latvia have gradually gotten under way."[71]

Helping Jews

From 2 July 1941 Jews all over Latvia were forbidden to stand in line at food stores. That amounted to a ban on buying food, as there always were lines. Thus Jews had to ask their Aryan friends, neighbors, or even complete strangers to buy food for them. This mercy effort worked, as there is no evidence of a serious famine among Jews in the few months they had left to live. Thousands of Latvians, mainly women, must have been involved.

The Jews paid their shoppers, sometimes generously. These "Jew supporters" as they were called in the press had to spend considerable time standing in line, often at several stores, as the amount sold to each buyer was limited. People whose shopping bags bulged often were reported to the police, which fined them and placed their names in the newspaper as "Jew Lovers" and "Traitors". Vestermanis, having himself received such help, contends that compassion and an urge to help, not monetary gain, were the main motives. His social circle changed: many former acquaintances limited their contacts with Jews or broke them off entirely. New faces took their place—people he barely knew or complete strangers—who offered their help unpretentiously, without many words.

Such a large-scale operation did not go unnoticed. Radio Rīga commented on 27 July: "Great is the number of compassionate Latvians who perform favors for Jews day after day. Often we hear: But that is a decent Jew." The tone of the press became ever more hysterical and threatening. "Tēvija" wrote on 15 October: "The friends of Jews must expect severe punishment." That meant arrest or even execution. The seamstress Adelīna Brodele in Alūksne was arrested because she had brought food for Jews and had loudly complained about the

---

[71] Ereignismeldung Nr. 40 of 1 August 1941.

persecution of Jews. She and her Jewish protégés were shot on 12 August. A farmer who had given a loaf of bread to German Jews was put in the Salaspils concentration camp where he perished in November 1943.

Tallying up Latvian Conduct

In the absence of public opinion polls it is difficult to determine the numbers of Latvians supporting or opposing the Holocaust—especially 70 years later. Nonetheless, we can get a few estimates.

Murderers and Accomplices. According to Ezergailis the total number was at most 3,000, with no more than 500 who actually „pulled the trigger".[72] The latter figure seems small at first glance, until one recalls that a mere 36 Germans working in 3 shifts killed some 25,000 Jews at Rumbula in two days. There Jeckeln wanted to demonstrate his efficiency by having murderers from his personal staff use submachine guns set for single shots, with only one bullet per victim. But even conventional killing methods, such as used by Karl Jäger's EK 3 in Daugavpils and Lithuania, enabled a few dozen German and Lithuanian murderers to kill up to 4,000 Jews in one day. As noted above, the number of accomplices may be higher by 1000 than Ezergailis' figure, but even 4,000 murderers and accomplices correspond to less than 0.3% of the Latvian population.

Rescuers and Helpers. There were at least 1,500 of them, or 0.1% of the population.

Informers or „Murderous anti-Semites". Two estimates can be made from the betrayals of Jews in hiding and their rescuers. One is based on the total number of arrested rescuers, the other, on Jews who changed hiding places at least 4 times, and thus had to evade a new set of potential informers at each place. Readers not interested in details of the calculation may skip the fine print below and merely note the results. They depend on N, the average number of people (neighbors, grocers, etc.) able to detect suspicious activity in the rescuer's apartment. For $N = 1, 2,$ or 3, the first method gives 9, 5, and 3% informers, and the

---

[72] Ezergailis, *Holocaust*, 21.

second, 5, 2.6, and 1.8%. In view of the crowded housing of wartime Latvia, *N* almost certainly was greater than 2, corresponding to less than 5% (or even 2.6%) of potential informers among Latvians.

(1) In an earlier section I cited Vestermanis' finding that 37 of some 400–450 rescuers were arrested, i.e. one in eleven. This number permits an estimate of the percentage of *murderous* anti-Semites (potential informers) among Latvians: fanatical enough to betray a fellow Latvian who sheltered Jews. Let *N* be the average number of people (neighbors, grocers, market vendors, mailmen, etc.) able to detect suspicious activity in the rescuer's apartment. Given that 1/11 of the rescuers were betrayed, the fraction of informers, *t*, in the population is 1/11*N*. If *N*=1, then *t*= 1/11 = 9%; if *N*=2, *t*= 1/22 = 5%; if *N*=3, *t*= 1/33 = 3%. Under the crowded conditions and limited privacy of wartime Latvia, *N* almost certainly was greater than 2, corresponding to less than 5% *murderous* anti-Semites.

This estimate is likely to be somewhat too high, as it counts each arrested rescuer as a single, independent event of betrayal. But the 6 rescuers arrested in Aizpute all came from a single event. A more accurate estimate will require a thorough analysis of the complete database.

(2) An independent estimate can be made from rescuer „networks". Žanis Lipke recruited 29 helpers, very few of whom were his close friends; some, especially those he recruited in Dobele, were complete strangers. Yet not one of them betrayed him. Israel Alīte and Abram Fleischmann in Liepāja stayed with 7 different hosts but were never caught. The hosts were not complete strangers to each other; each knew and trusted at least the previous and the next host. But at each address there were new neighbors and new passers-by, who could have seen or heard something. Even a slight suspicion if reported would have been followed up by the police. Thus Jews who moved from host to host faced new risks of betrayal with each move.

Vestermanis lists a number of Jews with multiple hosts: Eva Hoff (5 hosts), Serafima Paraša (4), Riva Schäfer (6), Valentina Freimane (7), Frida Michelsone (5), Haim Leibowitsch (4). To these we can add Alīte and Fleischmann in Liepāja (7 hosts). In these 38 hiding places there was only one threatened and one actual betrayal, or 1 out of 19. Proceeding as before, the fraction of informers, *t*, in the population is 1/19*N*, where *N* = average number of people able to detect the presence of a hidden Jew. For *N* = 1, 2, 3 the percentage of informers is 5%, 2.6%, and 1.8%. Again, these results could be refined by a detailed analysis of the database. Still, they are powerful evidence against the widely held stereotype that most Latvians were vicious anti-Semites.

An authoritative voice on this subject comes from historian Leo Dribins (b. 1931), professor at the University of Latvia. He survived the Holocaust because his mother was gentile, but he lost his father and all other Jewish relatives. Having lived in Latvia all his life, he surely has a well-founded opinion of the Latvian people. He writes:

„As an eyewitness and a history scholar I can confirm that the antisemitic propaganda hysteria of 1941 failed to influence the greatest part of the Latvian people. They rejected it. Some silently out of fear, others trying actively to resist Nazism and collaborators. Passive resistance was very widespread. The people's negative attitude toward the destruction of Jews is confirmed also by documents and memoirs of the Nazi occupiers. The acting Mayor of Rīga in 1941–44, [the German] Hugo Wittrock, writes in his [posthumous] memoirs that the majority of the people of Rīga were angered by the murder of Jews, condemning it and calling it a godless crime. The Liepāja District Commissioner Walter Alnor reported to his superior, General Commissioner Otto Drechsler, that the killing of Jews in Courland has caused great agitation among the people of Liepāja, and that German authority has suffered significantly. The SS and Police Chief in Liepāja on 3. January 1942 reported to his superior in Rīga that the people widely deplore the fate of Jews and that thus far only a few voices speak positively about the elimination of Jews. One rumor among others claims that the execution was filmed so as to have material in hand against the Latvian Auxiliary Police.

In the days after the massacre the mood in [Liepāja] Latvian society was gloomy and yet very upset. Many concluded that the ruthlessness of the Nazi regime will inevitably touch more and more Latvians.[73]“

Dribins' scholarly account is supported by a rare „grassroots" account—the unpublished diary of Jānis Jaunsleinis: Liepāja customs agent, union steward, and communist. Hidden for many years, the diary was transcribed in 1987 from the original handwritten notebooks. Here are two

[73] Dribins, Leo. *Antisemītisms un tā izpausmes Latvijā: Vēstures atskats* (Anti-Semitism in Latvia and its Manifestations in Latvia: Historic Review). Rīga: Institute of the History of Latvia, 2002. ISBN 9984–601–28–5.

excerpts from the days after the massacre of 15.–17. December 1941.

> „18.12.1941. The agitation in town is high. Never before during its existence has the city seen such mass murders. These horrors are too great for people to remain silent. Every decent person condemns the murderers and curses the „New European Order". But there is no lack of people who rub their hands in joy, grabbing the belongings of the exterminated people, emptying their abandoned apartments. But we cannot regard such degenerates as human.

> 25.12.1941. *[Christmas Day. With his wife and 2 children, Jaunsleinis squeezes into the hugely overcrowded narrow-gauge train to the countryside, where he and all others will visit relatives or friends hoping to get some foodstuffs, especially fats, by barter.]* „People are packed in the cars, like herring in a barrel. Nonstop chatter and hubbub in the front. No lack of people who have „fortified" themselves first thing in the morning. Two men in former home guard uniforms are pretty well sloshed. They brag to each other about their recent „heroic deeds", evidently at Šķēde. The other passengers sullenly turn away from this human trash, not wanting to listen to their disgusting stories. Suddenly from the other end of the carriage resounds a loud shout: „murderers!" Both ‚heroic' fascist henchmen fall silent and try to spot the brave man who had the courage to throw the truth in their faces. This time they did not succeed because the crowd was too dense."[74]

FIGHTING UNDER THE GERMAN FLAG

By the time the German army invaded the USSR on 22 June 1941, most Latvians were seething with rage at the Soviet occupiers. In one year, the occupiers had crushed Latvia's hard-won independence and by brazen fraud turned the country into a Soviet colony. They pauperized the prosperous country, terrorized the people by arresting, torturing, and killing its leaders and many other people, all the while force-feeding them Orwellian lies. The climax came on 14 June 1941, when more than 15 000 people were arrested in the middle of the night and deported to the Gulag or to perpetual exile in primitive regions of the Far North.

---

[74] Jaunsleinis, Jånis. Unpublished diary, 1941–44 (in Latvian). Transcribed by Staņislavs Korklišs. File MEL III 2503, Museum „Jews in Latvia," Rīga.

Many Latvians, fearing that they might be next, fled into the woods. When German troops crossed the border a week later, most Latvians greeted them as liberators, overcoming their distrust of this traditional enemy and expecting quick restoration of Latvian independence. Thousands of men volunteered to fight alongside the German army, but were rebuffed and disarmed. They did not know that Hitler had other plans for their country. On 16 July 1941 he had told a top-secret meeting of 5 leading Nazis at his headquarters: *We must never permit anybody but Germans to carry arms [west of the Urals]! ...The entire Baltic area must become Reich territory.*[75] He emphatically forbade formation of any "Legions" of East European nations.

Police Battalions

However, growing Soviet resistance in the battles for Smolensk (July–September 1941) and Moscow (October 1941– January 1942) and manpower shortages of the Army led to some second thoughts. Himmler found a loophole in Hitler's ban, permitting formation of Latvian combat units [initially] limited to no more than 501 men deceptively called "Auxiliary Police Battalions" and kept under his control rather than the Wehrmacht's. Starting in September 1941, such battalions were organized for anti-partisan and combat duty, recruited from existing municipal police as well as volunteers.[76] Their initial enlistment was for only 6 months, but by coercion it was then extended to the end of the war.

A major recruiting campaign started in February 1942, and by the time it ended in June 1942, 13 battalions comprising about 8,000 men had been formed. In the next 2 years, another 22 battalions were formed from conscripts. The total number was 42, including 5 Russian ones that were transferred to the Vlasov

---

[75] Unsigned Memorandum by Martin Bormann (16 July 1941), in United States Department of State, *Documents on German Foreign Policy, 1918–1945: From the Archives of the German Foreign Ministry.* Washington, DC: United States Government Printing Office, 1964. Series D (1937–1945), The War Years, Volume 13: June 23–December 11, 1941. Document Number 114 (Nuremberg Document 221-L), pp. 149–56.

[76] An excellent reference is Kārlis Kangeris, "'Closed' Units of Latvian Police— Lettische Schutzmannschafts-Bataillone: Research Issues and Pre-History". *Symposium* vol. 14, 2005, 104–121.

army in 1943 [the Russian Liberation Army (ROA), organized by Germany in WWII].

Soviet and post-Soviet publications have often accused Latvian police battalions of committing major war crimes during anti-partisan operations in Belarus and elsewhere. Nazi Germany completely ignored the Hague and Geneva conventions in anti-partisan operations behind the Eastern Front, and so the troops under its leadership—including Latvian police battalions—are potentially implicated in any war crimes during such operations.

Anti-partisan warfare as such is not necessarily a war crime. The 1907 Hague Convention requires that partisans wear uniforms or civilian clothes with prominent markings to qualify as *lawful combatants* like regular enemy soldiers, with all the rights of POWs prescribed by the Convention. However, partisans behind the Eastern Front although organized and commanded by Moscow,[77] wore no uniforms and if they had markings those generally were hard to see from a distance. Thus they fell outside the Convention (like the "unlawful combatants" captured by the US in Afghanistan and elsewhere). As described by Gerlach in his monumental book, the war was brutal, with neither partisans nor Nazi troops taking prisoners.[78] Worse still, it became a ruthless slaughter of civilians. Fearing to venture into the big forests where the partisans were hiding, Nazi troops in 1942 adopted the "cauldron" strategy, surrounding areas where partisans were active and burning down village after village suspected of supporting partisans. Failure to deliver its quota of farm products to the authorities was deemed sufficient proof of such support. Usually all villagers were killed and their livestock and grain were carried off.

Gerlach has estimated the total number of alleged partisans killed in Byelorussia as 345,000. German figures consistently

---

[77] Heinrihs Strods, *PSRS kaujinieki Latvijā (1941–1945)*, [USSR Combatants in Latvia (1941–1945)]. Rīga: LU žurnāla "Latvijas Vēsture" fonds, 2006 Part 1; 2007 Part 2.

[78] Christian Gerlach, *Kalkulierte Morde: Die deutsche Wirtschafts- und Vernichtungspolitik in Weißrußland 1941 bis 1944*. Hamburg: Hamburger Edition, 2000. ISBN 3930908638. Important parts of the text are available in English translation at http://rodohforum.yuku.com/topic/2482

show that for every weapon captured, about 10 people were killed. This suggests that only ~10% were partisans, the rest were villagers. Indeed, several high-ranking officials of the German civil administration came to the same conclusion, not believing the clumsy excuse of the SS that the partisans buried their weapons when capture seemed imminent.

A post-Soviet paper by Byelorussian historian Alexei Litvin discusses in detail the participation of Latvian police battalions in these atrocities.[79] He lists 26 battalions, but at least 6 of them (208, 231, 347, 432, 546, and 860) are unknown among Latvian units.[80] The error rate among his claims is high. His 39 sources include mostly German and Soviet documents, but some of the latter seem unreliable, particularly in regard to unit numbers, dates, numbers of victims, and even specifics of atrocities. During the war the Soviets surely had a detailed list of enemy units, so to give their reports greater credibility, they may have been tempted to assign specific unit numbers from that list when the actual number was not known.

For example, Litvin writes that 50 mainly Latvian SS-men under German command took part in the murder of 9,000 Jews in the Borisov ghetto in 1941, though Latvians were not eligible to serve even in affiliates of the Waffen-SS until 1943. He claims that special murder teams of „SS-men and Latvian volunteers" under German command helped kill 18,000 Jews in the Slonim area in the summer of 1942, and that the 18th Latvian police battalion took part in these murders. That account, as well as a 1959 NKVD trial of the 18th battalion, has been thoroughly examined by Ezergailis on the basis of NKVD trial records and daily records of the 18th Battalion in the Hoover Institution.[81] He finds that the killings of Jews attributed to Latvians most likely were carried out by Latvian SD units in the area, not by the 18th Battalion, which was deployed elsewhere on those dates.

---

[79] Alexey Litvin, "Latviešu policijas bataljoni Baltkrievijā 1941.–1944. gadā" (Latvian police battalions in Byelorussia 1941–1944). *Symposium*, vol. 2, 252–265.

[80] Kārlis Kangeris, *op. cit.*

[81] Ezergailis, *Nazi-Soviet Disinformation About the Holocaust in Nazi-Occupied Latvia.* Rīga: Latvijas 50 gadu okupācijas muzeja fonds, 2005, 41–56 (hereafter Ezergailis, *Disinformation*).

The most gruesome crimes that Litvin attributes to Latvians come from V. Baltiņš, a Latvian officer of the German-organized „Russian Liberation Army" under Gen. Vlasov. Baltiņš repeatedly traveled through Byelorussia in 1943/44 and sent reports to a Col. V. Pozdnyakov of Vlasov's army living in Rīga. He claims to have talked—in Latvian—to several Latvian „SS-men" in Morochkovo village on 23 April 1944, asking them why there were hundreds of bodies of women, children, and old people around the village. The alleged answer was „We killed them to eliminate as many Russians as possible". A sergeant then took him to a burned down house, pointed to several burned, half-buried corpses, and said „These we burned alive".

In the region of Kobylniki [Narach] village Baltiņš claims to have seen about 3,000 bodies as well as a number of severed heads in a barrel over which flies were circling. Surviving residents „left no doubt in his mind" that all this was done by Latvian SS. Burning people alive was an outrageous but all too common crime in German anti-partisan and anti-Jewish operations in Byelorussia, but the severed heads in a barrel, kept in the village by survivors, strain credibility. It may be part of the massive demonization campaign that the Soviets had launched against Latvians and other captive nations that dared fight against their oppressors. The Soviets severely punished captured members of Vlasov's army, but a native Latvian speaker like Baltiņš, able to speak to the „traitors" in their own language and so loosening their tongues, could be a useful propaganda tool. Baltiņš would not be the first Nazi collaborator to become an NKVD mouthpiece to save his hide. Whether by their own volition or upon coaching by the NKVD, such turncoats generally gave improbably lurid accounts of Nazi atrocities, although the plain truth would have been bad enough.

Litvin infers from captured German documents that about 150,000–200,000 soldiers were engaged in anti-partisan warfare in 1942. That included 5 Latvian police battalions, i.e. about 2,500 men or 1.2–1.7%. Without detailed data on their deployment and activities (including 1943–44) one cannot estimate how many deaths they were responsible for. But simple proportionality suggests that the number was in the thousands, perhaps even more than 10,000 if as many as 20 Latvian battalions were in Byelorussia for a year or longer. That is a serious stain on the record of Latvian police battalions. It is mitigated by the fact that they had volunteered not for slaughter of villagers but for frontline combat against the Red Army, which had robbed Latvia of her independence. Moreover, being under overall command of the German Waffen SS, their obedience was harshly enforced.

The "Volunteer" Latvian Waffen-SS Legion

As German losses on the Eastern Front mounted their need for additional manpower rose. From 1940 on, the SS had been accepting volunteers from other Germanic nations, soon organized into separate "Legions". Despite Hitler's early ban on non-Germanic legions, they were formed from late 1941 onward, roughly in the order of the Nazi racial hierarchy. Estonians, with a high percentage of blond people, got their Legion in October 1942, but Latvians, of whom only 2/3 were blond, had to wait until 10 February 1943, a week after the disastrous German defeat at Stalingrad where the 6th Army was destroyed with 841,000 casualties. Hitler now ordered formation of a *Latvian Volunteer SS Legion*. "Volunteer" was a camouflage term to circumvent the Hague Convention's ban of military conscription in occupied territories. Indeed, within days of Hitler's order, draft registration was announced in Latvia for men born between 1919 and 1924, and some men even received explicit *induction* notices.

The nucleus of the Legion was 6 police battalions that were in combat at Krasnoye Selo at the Leningrad front. In February 1943 battalions 16, 19, and 21 were merged into a *"1st Latvian Volunteer Regiment of the Waffen SS"* and sent into combat near Leningrad on 18 March 1943.[82] Next battalions 18, 24, and 26 were merged into a 2nd Regiment. The two regiments, greatly augmented by draftees, later became the *15th* and *19th Division of the Waffen SS*. Contrary to an early promise, each division was commanded by a German rather than a Latvian general and had a German staff; the highest ranking Latvians were regimental commanders.

---

[82] Ezergailis, *Disinformation*. 60–63.

By the time the Latvian divisions were deployed at full strength in 1943/44, Army Group North was on the defensive and eventually in retreat. The Latvian divisions often were used as rear guard, with heavy losses. The 15th division was so decimated in 1944 (some regiments were reduced to 200 men) that it was sent to East Prussia and then to West Prussia to be reconstituted. Still not combat-ready and short of equipment, it fought the Soviet Army in early 1945 but in the last month of the war it retreated westward against German orders, enabling most of its units to surrender to the Western Allies. The 19th Division remained in Latvia with the German 16th and 18th Armies, defending "Fortress Courland" until the very end of the war.

The International Military Tribunal in Nuremberg in its verdict of 1 October 1946 ruled both the *Allgemeine* (General) *SS* and the *Waffen SS* to be criminal organizations. However, they exempted draftees of both the German and foreign Waffen-SS units:

«...excluding, however, those who were drafted into membership by the State in such a way as to give them no choice in the matter, and who had committed no such crimes.»[83]

In 1950 the US Displaced Persons' Commission extended this exemption specifically to the Baltic Legions:

«...That the Baltic Waffen-SS Units (Baltic Legions) are to be considered as separate and distinct in purpose, ideology, activities, and qualifications for membership from the German SS, and therefore the Commission holds them not to be a movement hostile to the Government of the United States under Section 13 of the Displaced Persons Act, as amended.»[84]

Nonetheless, the Russian Government and a number of Western media ignore this distinction and continue to depict the Latvian Legion as a murder gang equal to the worst of the German Waffen-SS. Moreover, they call all 3 uniformed branches "Latvian SS Legion" despite their greatly different levels of guilt of the Latvian SD (high level), police battalions (intermediate

---

[83] *Trial of the Major War Criminals before the International Military Tribunal, Nuremberg, 14 November 1945–1 October 1946.* Vol. XXII. Nuremberg: International Military Tribunal (1948), 517.

[84] Letter by Commissioner Harry N. Rosenfield to Dr. J. Feldmanis, Chargé d'affaires of Latvia, 12 September 1950. Quoted from A. Ezergailis, *The Latvian Legion.* Rīga: Historical Institute of Latvia (1997), 93–94.

level) and Legion (low level). Although a fraction of the legionnaires had blood on their hands from prior service in police battalions and other uniformed units that is no reason to stigmatize the Legion as such. Being deployed only in frontline combat, its involvement in war crimes was no greater than that of hundreds of *Wehrmacht* divisions, to say nothing of Soviet Army divisions.[85]

War Crimes by and War Criminals in the Legion

There is no question that some war criminals served in the Legion. As mentioned before, the original nucleus of the Legion was 6 police battalions that had served on the Leningrad front until early 1943. Additional police battalions were absorbed into the Legion later on, and some of them undoubtedly had been involved in atrocities in Byelorussia. Moreover, some members of the Latvian SD and auxiliary police who had killed Jews in 1941 later volunteered for or were conscripted into police battalions, bringing along their taint. But most members of the SD and police had managed to avoid service outside Latvia, preferring cushy jobs as camp guards or policemen. (Indeed, NKVD interrogation records show that a number of volunteers who joined the Arājs Commando in 1942–44 had done so mainly to avoid military duty.[86]) In late 1944, after the partisan areas had been liberated by the Soviet Army, the Arājs Commando itself was dispersed into the decimated 15th Division in Pomerania. The civilian population there was German, keeping the Arājs men from engaging in their vaunted mass murder skills.

Only one war crime has been attributed to the Latvian Legion:

---

[85] The Lithuanian writer Balys Sruoga (1896–1947) who was a political prisoner writes that some Latvian legionnaires served as guards at Stutthof and were notorious for their cruelty. [Balys Sruoga, *Dievų miškas* (Forest of the Gods)]. Chicago, 1957. 482 p.). A likely explanation is that a company of the Arājs Commando arrived in Germany in late summer of 1944 and was to be dissolved. Just then Stutthof was receiving many thousands of prisoners evacuated from Latvia and Lithuania, and presumably needed more guards. The Arājs men were much better qualified for this task than young draftees, and because of their very similar uniforms could have been mistaken for legionnaires.

[86] Vīksne, *Arājs Commando.*

"At Podgaje [Flederborn], 2 February 1945, men of [the 15th] division performed a war crime on Polish prisoners, burning in a barn 32 soldiers from 4th Co, 3rd Inf Regt, 1st [Kościuszko] Div Polish First Army, tied up with a barbed wire."[87]

This charge is based on a 1945 investigation by the Polish Army, summarized in English by Juergen Fritz.[88] Mr. Fritz has reviewed much of the available information, including the book by *Oberführer* Arturs Silgailis (Chief of Staff of the 15th Div)[89] and two war diaries and a book by *Sturmbannführer* Jūlijs Ķīlītis, (Commander of 1 Bn 34th Regt that fought Polish troops at Podgaje on 31 Jan),[90] posts on various military forums, and the 1979 film *Elegia,* based in part on the account of the sole survivor, ensign Zbigniew Furgała.[91] My own assessment, agreeing largely with that of Mr. Fritz, is that the Polish Army report contains a major mistake along with smaller ones: it conflates *two* battles on 31 Jan 1945 into *one!*

The **first battle** occurred in *daylight* at 14:30–15 h, when 1 Bn 3 Rgt of the Polish 1 Div approached Podgaje and was attacked by the defenders—Battalion 2 of the German/Dutch *SS-Panzergrenadier-Regiment 48, „General Seyffart".* The Polish battalion withdrew after a firefight, but the 4th Co was cut off and suffered heavy losses. The last 37 men surrendered after they had run out of ammunition. The Panzergrenadiers locked them in a barn in Podgaje. There were no Latvians yet in Podgaje during the firefight; they still were 3–4 hours away.

Around midnight several German SS-officers appeared in the barn and began to take men out for interrogation, who returned beaten and bloodied. Fearing to be shot, 5 POWs overpowered or killed a guard and escaped. Ski troops gave chase and killed 4 of the escapees but Furgała got away and was able to return to his unit. No eyewitness reports exist for subsequent events, but

---

[87] http://en.wikipedia.org/wiki/15th_Waffen_Grenadier_Division_of_the_SS_(1st_Latvian) and references therein. See also http://lwp.armiam.com/historyLWP.html

[88] Juergen Fritz, http://tinyurl.com/6cuo5dm and posts in other forums.

[89] Silgailis, Arturs, *Latvian Legion*. San Jose: R.J. Bender (1986).

[90] Ķīlītis, Jūlijs, *Es karā aiziedams: mani raksturīgākie piedzīvojumi Otrā pasaules karā.* [Going to war—my most distinctive experiences during the Second World War. UK: Published by the author (1956), 279 pp.

[91] http://www.dws.org.pl/; http://www.szczecinek.org/forum/; http://forum.panzer-archiv.de.

apparently on the SS-officers' orders, the 32 remaining POWs were shot the same night. That had been frequent practice of the Waffen-SS, especially on the Eastern Front.

Artillery and tank fire on Podgaje steadily intensified in the next days, climaxing with a major assault on 3 Feb when 90% of the buildings including the wooden barn burned down, whereupon the village was captured at about 11 h. Polish troops found the burnt remains of their bound comrades and assumed that they were deliberately burned alive that morning. No autopsies were performed, only a visual inspection by a physician and a political commissar 2 days later, concluding that the blisters on some partly burned bodies implied that the victims were burned alive. Actually burn blisters do form on dead bodies, but unless formed soon after death, they do not show the red margins that often appear on living tissue.[92] But the report does not mention red margins. A later report by a political commissar mentions bullet holes in some of the skulls. A detailed analysis by Fritz and Anders (paper in press) concludes that the POWs most likely were shot during the first night and had been dead for two days when the barn caught fire.

The **second battle** occurred in *darkness* at about 19 h on 31 Jan. Three decimated battalions of the Latvian 34 and 32 regiments had left Jastrowie at 14 h to relieve the Podgaje garrison. Coming under fire they had to leave the road and continue in deep snow across fields and forests, some time after 18 h finally reaching an open field within sight of Podgaje. A Polish POW who had fallen off a tank told them that 2 Polish battalions just then were stealthily advancing toward Podgaje to capture it by surprise. Ķīlītis' battalion quickly followed but suddenly was met by heavy fire. In the ensuing firefight the Polish battalions suffered casualties and lost about 95 POWs, but most of their men scattered in the darkness and escaped. Approaching Podgaje, the Latvians at first were met by fierce „friendly fire" as the garrison thought they were enemies. Once that mistake was cleared up, the Latvians turned over the POWs to the 48. SS Panzergrenadier Regt. All 3 Latvian battalions then were allowed to enter Podgaje, but only single-file.

An hour after arriving in Podgaje at 21 h, Major Ķīlītis toured the village and its defense perimeter. He saw "many corpses of

---

[92] http://tinyurl.com/4zyjscu

people and cattle in the streets, including Polish POWs shot by the Germans". The 1 Polish Division had crossed the German frontier only on 29 Jan and first approached Podgaje only a few hours ago, in the first battle of 31 Jan. All 37 POWs captured in that battle were still in the barn, awaiting interrogation. Thus the dead POWs Ķīlītis saw that evening must have been the very 95 he had captured that evening—shot only an hour or two ago!

It is virtually certain that the Latvians did not kill the 37, let alone the 95. On arrival they were assigned quarters and presumably food, but then were ordered to take the night watch on the defense perimeter, relieving the 2nd battalion of *SS-Freiwilligen-Panzergrenadier-Brigade Nederland, Regiment 48 "General Seyffardt"*. These troops, perhaps also German units such as *Kampfgruppe Scheibe* under *SS-Ostubaf* Siegfried Scheibe, were available for the killing. Ķīlītis was not present at the interrogations but reports in his diary and book being shocked to learn from the German officers the next day that the prisoners had been killed.

Given the Nazis' extreme disdain for Slavs it is conceivable that the Latvian Legion was involved in some war crimes on the Eastern Front—on German orders or as spontaneous reprisals. The Soviets had every opportunity to investigate any such war crimes, as a sizable fraction of the 15th Div surrendered to them in Germany at the end of the war, as did the last remnants of the 19th Div in Kurzeme. The Soviets then detained men of military age in special „filtration camps" for up to several years, where they were scrutinized under presumption of guilt and coercion to implicate others. Although the Soviets sent many legionnaires to the Gulag and Russia still maligns them as a murder gang equal to the German Waffen-SS, the only trials the Soviets conducted were against members of police battalions 18 and 21, not against members of the Legion. These trials, for killings of Jews and other civilians in Byelorussia and in Liepāja, have been criticized by Ezergailis as show trials,[93] although at least some of the defendants appear to have been guilty.

---

[93] Ezergailis, *Disinformation*. 45–51.

For Hitler or Against Stalin?

Germans had been the traditional enemy of the Latvian people, ruling and exploiting them for centuries. This enmity is well established in the Latvian literary tradition. But when Nazi Germany invaded the USSR, many Latvians greeted them as liberators. A year before, Stalin had brutally robbed Latvia of its hard-earned independence, terrorized and impoverished the country, and deported more than 1% of the population to the Gulag or to perpetual exile in Siberia. Even a number of Jews, including my own family, welcomed Germans as the lesser evil. Many Latvians expected Germany quickly to restore Latvian sovereignty.

For Jews the rude awakening came almost instantly, when Einsatzgruppen started the Holocaust. For Latvians the disenchantment took longer, as the war, with stiffening Soviet resistance, seemed to justify—for the time being—the German decision to keep power in German hands. Most Latvians disapproved to varying degrees of the mass murder of Jews, but for many this was tempered by the realization that little Latvia alone could never defeat the Soviet oppressors; only Nazi Germany was strong enough to do so. By the old principle, "the enemy of my enemy is my friend", many Latvians chose to side with Germany and fight under the Nazi flag as volunteers or draftees.

This was exactly the same choice made by Finland in 1941. Faced with Soviet demands in 1939, she had chosen to fight and by valiant resistance succeeded in keeping her sovereignty despite substantial losses of territory. When Germany attacked the USSR in 1941 Finland promptly joined the fight. But there were two major differences. (1) Finland still had her government and army in 1941 and was able to limit her alliance with Germany to military matters alone. Finnish troops fought under their own flag, their own generals, and their own code of conduct as well as in their own uniforms. When it became increasingly obvious that Germany was losing the war, Finland abrogated the alliance in September 1944 and negotiated a truce with the USSR. (2) Finland had only a small Jewish population and was able to protect it from persecution, although under Nazi pressure it surrendered 8 Jews with foreign citizenship.

Latvians, who had been robbed of their independence by the Soviets, surely had as great a right as the Finns to fight on the side of Germany. Both were fighting against Stalin, not for Hitler! Nobody condemns the Finns for fighting against this murderous tyrant and nobody should condemn the Latvians for also fighting against him—just because they were forced to serve under Nazi flags and generals, wearing Nazi uniforms and SS insignia.

There are some moral burdens applying to Latvians but not Finns. A crushing burden falls on the Latvian SD (peak strength ~1200 members), which committed or abetted some 60,000 murders in Latvia and Byelorussia, more than half of them Jews. They also served as concentration camp guards. Many though not all of the police battalions (peak strength ~12,000 members) were involved in brutal anti-partisan warfare in Byelorussia, and although they were acting under German orders, that does not absolve them of all guilt. Other police battalions were engaged only in frontline combat. Lastly, the Legion (nominal strength 52,000) also did mainly frontline combat, with scant evidence of involvement in atrocities.

JUDGING LATVIANS, JUDGING LATVIA

Even fruit flies and octopuses have distinctive personalities and behaviors.[94] Yet billions of people—especially in the Third World—judge others not by their individual conduct and character but by rigid stereotypes based on race, tribe, or religion. Regrettably this mode of thought is all too common also among Jews. Having all been tarred with the same brush by Hitler, one might expect them to be more objective, judging people by their *individual* actions and character. Instead a tribal mentality is widespread: refusing to shake hands with a young

---

[94] Jennifer A. Mather, Roland C. Anderson, and James B. Wood, *Octopus: The Ocean's Intelligent Invertebrate*. Portland: Timber, 2010; Charles Siebert, "The Animal Self". *New York Times*, 22 January, 2006; Gosling, S. D. "From mice to men: What can we learn about personality from animal research?" *Psychological Bulletin*, 127, 45-86, 2001.

Lithuanian, refusing to buy a German car, and condemning *all* Latvians, Poles, Ukrainians, etc. as anti-Semites.

This attitude is not uncommon even among Latvian Jews, including some whose lives were saved by Latvians. Bernhard Press and his father Oskar were hidden by Professor Artūrs Krūmiņš and his family for 3 years, but he later wrote a book claiming that *"most of the intelligentsia, together with the majority of the Latvian people, were entirely in favor of the "elimination" of the Jews and not only encouraged the mob to shed blood but also actively participated themselves."*[95] He personally witnessed some persecutions in the summer and fall of 1941 before finding shelter with the Krūmiņš family, and he reports many second-hand accounts, a number of which are credible. But though trained as an MD, he is shockingly uncritical and biased: trusting discredited sources (Extraordinary Commission reports, false or misinterpreted quotes by Jeckeln, a 1938 picture of a burning German synagogue claimed to be from Rīga 1941), inferring interregnum killings from the difference of two poorly known large numbers (a most elementary mistake in science!) or from mixing numbers and facts from Lithuania and Latvia, etc. An extenuating circumstance is Soviet persecution after "liberation": father Oskar committed suicide and son Bernhard spent years in the Gulag before being permitted to emigrate to Germany. A condition of his release may have been to serve as a mouthpiece of Soviet propaganda. It is regrettable that the English translation of 2000 ignores the enormously important work by Ezergailis, Vestermanis, and others published after the 1992 German edition of Press.

Several of the stereotypers accusing most or all Latvians are quite religious, but seem to have forgotten the Old Testament story of Sodom and Gomorrah. When Abraham pleaded with the Lord to spare these two sinful cities, the Lord agreed to do so if Abraham could find 10 righteous men among the residents. Abraham couldn't, and so the two cities were destroyed after Abraham's nephew Lot had been granted free passage. The total

---

[95] Press, Bernhard, *Judenmord in Lettland 1941–1945*. Berlin: Metropol, 1992; *ibid.*, *The Murder of the Jews in Latvia 1941-1945*. Evanston: Northwestern University Press. 2000.

population of these cities is not known, but even if it had been as small as 1000,[96] the Lord's demand amounted to only 1%. From the evidence presented earlier in this Part, well over half the Latvians in WWII were decent, thus greatly over-fulfilling the Lord's quota.

Prosecuting Guilty Men

Crimes are committed by individuals, not nations. Such individuals were prosecuted in East and West after WWII, but by opposite norms.

In the West, the principle was "innocent until proven guilty", often leading to the decision not to indict because the evidence seemed insufficient, or even to some undeserved acquittals or releases though the evidence was strong. (The 1949 release by Britain of arch-murderer Viktors Arājs is a glaring example.) The best-studied case is German Reserve Police Battalion 101, which had shot at least 38,000 Jews and deported 45,200 to the Treblinka death camp.[97] Of 210 men interrogated by the Hamburg prosecutors, 14 were indicted and 11 convicted, but only two served prison terms (of 4 and 3½ years) after appeal. Most other German police battalions were never investigated or indicted. A few Latvians were put on trial in the US and Canada, but most were acquitted for lack of evidence, and a few others died during the trial. The most seriously implicated defendant was SD-man Kārlis Detlavs, but he was acquitted because the prosecution had botched the indictment out of ignorance about conditions in occupied Latvia.[98] Although it is deplorable that most war criminals in the West escaped prosecution, that is the price we have to pay for the principle „innocent until proven guilty".

In the East, a different principle prevailed: "guilty if the state says so". (Even today, 99% of non-jury trials in Russia end in

---

[96] For what it is worth, extensive archeological excavations reported by biblical literalists suggest a population of 600–1200 for these two cities. (http://www.accuracyingenesis.com/sodom.html)

[97] Browning Christopher R., *Ordinary Men: Reserve Police Battalion 101 and the Final Solution in Poland,* New York: Harper 1992, 225–226.

[98] Ezergailis, *Disinformation,* 188.

convictions.[99]) There are countless examples of Jews liberated from concentration camps whom the NKVD sent to the Soviet Gulag on the assumption that any Jew who survived must have spied for, collaborated with, or bribed the Nazis.[100] The formal charges were „Treason Against Homeland" under the dreaded Art. 58–1a, or when this was untenable, „Socially Dangerous Element" under Art. 7–35.

Some people may find comfort in the fact that the same ruthless NKVD machine that swept up many innocent Jews also swept up many Latvian men, including all those that were of military age during the German occupation. Some eventually were released, the others were sent to prison or Gulag, including most of the guilty but also many of the innocent.

These two norms are often stated in hyperbolical form as „Better let 100 guilty go free than convict an innocent" and its converse. One can argue whether the ratio should be 10:1 or even 1:1, but in the specific case of WWII crimes by Latvians, overly lenient justice has been less of a problem than complete evasion of justice. Most of the Latvian war criminals that got to the West before the end of the war were safe from prosecution. Few fellow Latvians knew of their crimes, and some of them were reluctant to turn against fellow refugees who had lost their homeland. Other Latvians did have the courage to identify war criminals (such as those POWs who twice identified Arājs to British authorities or the refugee who gave me the names of a dozen Latvians who had killed Jews), but such tips stopped after being ignored by authorities. Most Latvians left Germany long before German courts began serious efforts to prosecute non-Germans, and once they got to their new countries they had bigger worries than—obviously futile—reporting of suspected war criminals.

There is no statute of limitations on murder. But with each passing decade prospects of finding and successfully prosecuting war criminals become dimmer. Realistically one must balance the need to punish the murderers against the need to protect the innocent and the obstacles to getting convictions that are fully exploited by defense lawyers: fading memories of

---

[99] Glenn E. Curtis, ed. *Russia: A Country Study*. Washington: GPO for the Library of Congress, 1996; Peter Finn, "Fear Rules in Russia's Courtrooms," *Washington Post*, 27 February 2005, p. A01.

[100] Irēne Šneidere, Politiskās prāvas pret ebrejiem Latvijā 1944.–1952. gadā (*Political Trials Against Jews in Latvia 1944–1952*). *Symposium* vol. 2, 328–349.

witnesses, public sympathies for old pajama-clad men in wheelchairs, revulsion against bounties offered by Efraim Zuroff on behalf of the Wiesenthal Center. Protecting the innocent is a valid concern in view of past miscarriages of justice, such as perjured testimony by Jewish survivors in the 1949/50 trials of the "Jewish SS-Officer" Fritz Scherwitz.[101]

Now, nearly 70 years after the murders, it is appropriate to take a fresh look at the problem. The victims are dead, and not even the most draconian punishment of the murderers will revive them. On the other hand, sending an innocent to prison or the gallows merely creates a new injustice. Would the victims want that? For ordinary murderers, punishment serves three purposes: retribution, deterrence, and protection of society. The last two are rarely an issue with war criminals who were motivated by hatred or by higher orders. In peacetime most of them masterfully control their hatred, becoming model citizens whose neighbors vouch for them—especially when the murderer has become old and frail. A significant number of mass murderers suffer mental breakdowns or nightmares, but that's not a sufficient punishment as Holocaust survivors do too. The most realistic approach may be that used by prosecutors: bring war criminals to justice whenever there is a fair chance of obtaining a conviction, but let the others go. Even if put on trial their lawyers will skillfully challenge any charges, leaving the public with the impression that the Holocaust has been greatly exaggerated. It is better to use the resources for Holocaust education and remembrance, especially in ex-communist countries where 3 generations were brought up in an atmosphere of Holocaust denial and crass distortions of history.

Guilty Nation?

Many critics who condemn Latvian involvement in Holocaust murders and in anti-partisan warfare (~4,000 including accomplices in the former and no more than 10,000 in the latter, i.e. ~1% of the Latvian population) extend the blame to the entire Latvian nation. They forget that Latvia had no government under German occupation. Whereas occupied Western European countries were nominally sovereign under a "Quisling" cabinet of ministers with a German civilian pulling

---

[101] Anita Kugler, *Scherwitz: Der jüdische SS-Offizier*. Cologne: Kiepenheuer & Witsch, 2004, 758 pp.

strings behind the scenes, Latvia had not a shred of sovereignty left, being ruled by Germans: *Generalkomissar Lettland* under a *Reichskomissar Ostland*, who often were overshadowed by the mighty *Höherer SS-und Polizeiführer Ostland*, Friedrich Jeckeln. As a magnanimous concession Latvia was allowed a puppet "self-administration" (not government) composed of "directors general" (not ministers).

Even the top German civilian, Reichskomissar Lohse, argued in vain in the summer of 1941 against the killing of Jews by the SD, as documented by Ezergailis.[102] German control over Latvia was very strong, as illustrated by the mantra in several German police documents: "German police are command organs, Latvian police are implementation organs". Every police precinct had at least one German liaison officer, as did every police battalion. It is absurd to blame the entire Latvian nation for crimes committed by 1% of its people but condemned by the majority.

After Latvia regained her independence in 1991, all her presidents have repeatedly condemned and apologized for the Latvian role in the Holocaust. An example is the words of President Vaira Vīķe-Freiberga at the dedication of the Memorial Wall in 2004 (translated from Latvian):

> „... Today, standing here at the memorial site for the victims of Nazism, it is important for everyone to understand and evaluate the events of that time. What madness and hatred had seized people that caused them to destroy thousands of innocent fellow men? Clearly, in a democratic state, as now is Latvia, one must openly, honestly, and forthrightly speak about one's past; know it and reevaluate it. To ensure that the events of the Nazi occupation of Latvia never happen again, there are important steps we must take: reject prejudices and intolerance among peoples, ban ethnic hatreds, and condemn expressions of anti-Semitism in any form whatsoever."

Three generations of Latvians have been born since 1945. None of them bear any responsibility for the murders committed by 1% of their compatriots during WWII. Recriminations and guilt trips are counter-productive, causing at best denial and ignorance of past history, and at worst, anti-Semitism.

---

[102] Ezergailis, *Holocaust*, 378.

INDEX